From Brenda's Kitchen
100 Favourite Recipes

From Brenda's Kitchen
100 Favourite Recipes

BRENDA COSTIGAN

Gill & Macmillan Ltd
Hume Avenue, Park West, Dublin 12
with associated companies throughout the world
www.gillmacmillan.ie

© Brenda Costigan 2009
Photographs: Property of *Sunday Independent* Life magazine
Photographer: Tony Gavin, *Sunday Independent*

978 07171 4561 4

Index compiled by Cover to Cover
Design by Graham Thew
Printed by GraphyCems, Spain

This book is typeset in 10pt Bembo on 13pt.

The paper used in this book comes from the wood pulp of managed forests.
For every tree felled, at least one tree is planted, thereby renewing natural
resources.

A CIP catalogue record for this book is available from the British Library.

5 4 3 2 1

To the newest members of our family, Ethan and Alex Swan and Rebecca McDonald, hoping that they will love to cook.

Contents

Acknowledgments

I wish to thank Aengus Fanning, the Editor of the *Sunday Independent*.

I also wish to thank Brendan O'Connor, Editor of the *Sunday Independent* Life magazine, for his permission to use the photographs in this book, which were first printed with my weekly column. Thanks to Tony Gavin for taking the lovely photographs and for his helpful advice during our numerous shoots.

Sincere thanks to Mary O'Sullivan, Features Editor of the *Sunday Independent*, for her constant help and guidance.

I thank Mary Shanahan for her typing skills and her ability to understand my hieroglyphics.

I wish to thank Sarah Liddy of Gill & Macmillan for her guidance. Also thanks to her team, Kristin Jensen, Aoife O'Kelly and Jane Rogers, for their skills, not forgetting the designers.

Thanks to my own family for their support: Catherine, Peter and David, and their spouses, David Swan, Helen Warner and Aoife FitzGerald. Thanks also to my sister Mary and her husband, Jim O'Donnell, for their advice.

Last but not least, thanks to my husband, Dick, who makes it possible.

Introduction

I hope you enjoy the recipes that I have included in this book. They are some of my favourites that I have featured in the *Sunday Independent* Life magazine over the past few years.

Selecting recipes isn't an easy task, but I've included a wide range, from starters to desserts. All have been family and friend tested and most of the ingredients should be easily available.

When you consider just how many meals we eat in our lifetime, it's a happy thing if we can enjoy cooking and eating them. For that reason, too, it's good to keep an eye on the need for a healthy diet.

Olive oil is my favourite fat to use, and even though it's often not explicitly called for in the recipes, I use an extra virgin (not too fruity) olive oil most of the time. I like to use butter for baking but will use polyunsaturated margarine for spreading and sometimes for making sauces and adding to mashed vegetables.

Freshly ground black pepper is a must in my kitchen. The flavour is so good and it helps me to use less salt.

I use fresh herbs whenever I can, but dried herbes de Provence and oregano are a great standby. I love fresh root ginger and I make sure to always have ground coriander, ground nutmeg and ground chilli powder in my kitchen as well. I could go on, but suffice it to say that I hope you enjoy the recipes as much as I do.

BRENDA

CHAPTER 1

Breakfast and Eggs

Waking up on a cold winter's morning, one could be forgiven for thinking that hibernation isn't a bad idea. However, getting out of bed can be greatly helped by the promise of a good hot breakfast. Attitudes to breakfast vary widely, even within one household, but we occasionally need to be reminded that research shows that, nutritionally speaking, breakfast is regarded as an important meal, especially for children. A sensible breakfast also helps prevent the temptation to eat snacks, which are usually high in fat and sugar.

Happily, a sensible breakfast can be quite simple, such as a bowl of porridge or other cereal with some fresh fruit. 'Go to work on an egg', that iconic catch-phrase from way back when, still stands. Countless studies have shown that a daily helping of oats is a good choice, particularly for the heart, because the type of fibre in oats sticks to 'bad' cholesterol and removes it from the body, thereby preventing it from clogging the arteries. Oats are excellent for making porridge (a handy and economical breakfast) and are the base of muesli. They can also be used in baking bread or biscuits or as a coating for fried fish.

Fruity Muesli

Serves 1

Your favourite brand of muesli or other cereal can be used as a base for this healthy breakfast. If preferred, simply use standard porridge oat flakes, which can be eaten straight from the packet because they have already been cooked as part of the preparation process. If you would like them to be crispier, see the note below. Fruits can vary according to season and availability.

You will need per serving:

1–2 scoops muesli

1 small banana, sliced

1 tablespoon blueberries

2–3 strawberries, halved

1 nectarine, unpeeled and chopped

1 tablespoon raisins

**1 tablespoon nuts (hazelnut, almonds, walnuts, etc.), raw or toasted
and coarsely chopped**

juice of 1 orange

1 x 150 ml (5 fl oz) carton fruit yoghurt (try strawberry)

a little milk, if necessary

1   Put the cereal into a generous-sized cereal bowl and mix in all the fruits and nuts. Moisten to taste with the orange juice, yoghurt and milk. Serve in pretty glass bowls.

NOTE: TO MAKE OAT FLAKES CRUNCHY AND CRISPY, PREHEAT THE OVEN TO 180°C/350°F/GAS 4. SPREAD THE OAT FLAKES IN A FAIRLY THIN LAYER OVER TWO OR MORE BAKING SHEETS AND BAKE FOR 5 MINUTES OR SO, UNTIL CRISPY. STIR THEM ONCE OR TWICE DURING BAKING SO THEY CRISP EVENLY. ALLOW TO COOL COMPLETELY, THEN STORE IN AN AIRTIGHT CONTAINER TO USE WHEN REQUIRED.

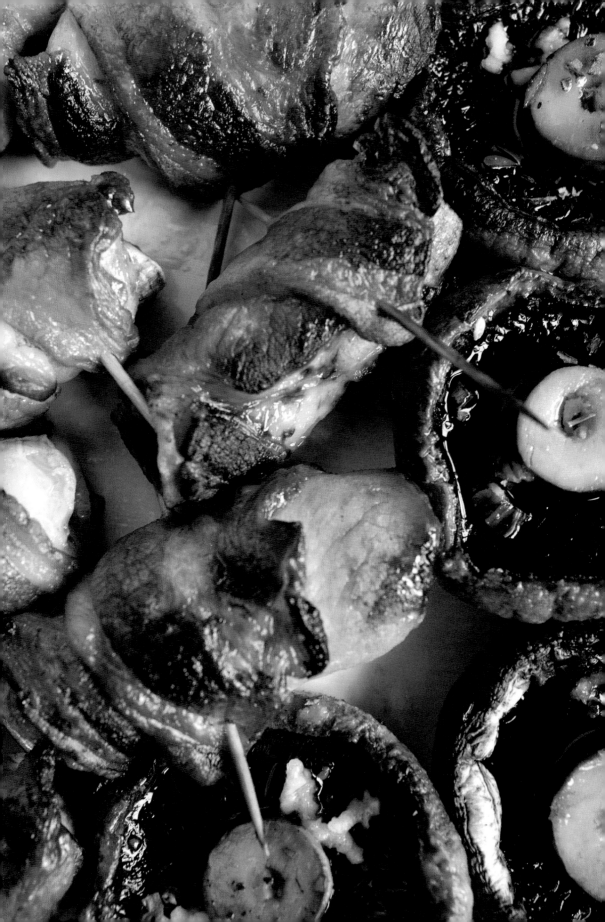

Banana Roll-ups

Serves 1

Bananas wrapped in rashers are a delightful combination of flavours.

You will need per serving:
1 banana
2–3 rashers
wooden cocktail sticks

1 Cut bananas into two or three pieces, depending on how large they are.
2 Wrap a rasher around each banana section, making sure the rasher overlaps itself on the banana just enough to cover the flesh (if exposed, the banana turns an unappetising grey under the grill). Hold the rashers in place with a number of wooden cocktail sticks, as they will curl up under the heat of the grill.
3 Grill for 6–8 minutes, turning on all sides, until golden. Serve hot.

NOTE: IF THE RASHERS ARE VERY LONG, CUT OFF ANY EXCESS, AS TOO MUCH RASHER WRAPPED ROUND AND ROUND THE BANANA WILL NEVER GET NICE AND CRISPY.

Slow-baked Flat Mushrooms

Serves 6

Treat yourself with this recipe, using the big flat mushrooms with velvety gills. They are the largest stage of growth of the common white mushroom. In this recipe they are baked slowly with olive oil, lemon juice and soy sauce. The resulting flavour is deliciously smooth and meaty. Serve them as part of a mixed grill. One per person should be sufficient, depending on the size, though they do shrink just a little.

You will need:

6 large flat mushrooms, stalks trimmed if necessary

40 g (1 ½ oz) butter

juice of ½–1 lemon, to taste

2–3 tablespoons olive oil

salt and freshly ground black pepper

2 cloves of garlic, crushed

a few sprigs of fresh thyme (or a light sprinkling of dried herbes de Provence)

1 Preheat the oven to 180°C/350°F/gas 4.
2 Wipe the mushrooms to get rid of turf mould, etc. – do not wash them.
3 Melt the butter in a pan and add in the mushrooms, rounded side down, and fry gently for 1–2 minutes. Transfer the mushrooms to a roasting tin or ovenproof dish, arranging them in a single layer. Spoon some of the melted butter over the mushrooms and pour the rest into the tin. Shake the lemon juice all over the mushrooms, followed by the olive oil. Season with salt and plenty of pepper. Scatter the garlic into and tuck the sprigs of thyme under the mushrooms, or if using the herbes de Provence, sprinkle it onto the mushrooms.
4 Cover the tin with foil and bake for about 30–45 minutes, removing the foil for the last 10 minutes of cooking.

Variation:

To serve as a starter, place each cooked mushroom on a circle of buttered toast (cut out with a scone cutter). If liked, butter the toast with a little garlic and herb cream cheese. Garnish with tiny sprigs of thyme.

Mexican Scramble

Serves 2

A tasty variation on scrambled egg. Chopped tomatoes and a little chopped chilli are included in the scrambled egg mixture, which is served on flour tortillas that are first fried quickly on both sides in a little oil, making them delightfully crispy.

You will need:

3–4 large eggs

4–5 tablespoons milk (less than usual because of the tomatoes)

salt and freshly ground black pepper

15 g ('/2 oz) butter

2 teaspoons olive oil

3 medium tomatoes, chopped

'/2 small red chilli, very thinly sliced, or '/4 teaspoon hot chilli powder

2 flour tortillas

a little oil to fry (optional)

To serve:

chopped fresh coriander or parsley

1 Whisk the eggs and milk together and season with salt and pepper. Set aside.
2 Melt the butter in the saucepan along with the oil. Add the chopped tomatoes and chilli and cook for a few minutes to soften, seasoning them lightly with salt and pepper.
3 Meanwhile, in a separate frying pan, fry each tortilla quickly on both sides until golden brown. Keep warm.
4 Mix the egg mixture into the hot cooked tomato mixture. Stir gently until the egg has started to cook. Draw off the heat before completely cooked, as the egg will continue to cook in its own heat.
5 Fry the tortillas in a dry pan (or with a little oil for a crisp finish) until lightly browned on both sides.
6 Spoon the scrambled egg and tomato mixture into the middle of each tortilla and scatter generously with the chopped coriander or parsley. Serve immediately.

Scrambled Eggs

Serves 1

This is such a simple dish, but it's frequently overcooked to the point of rubberiness. The perfect scrambled egg should have a wonderful creaminess to it. This is easily achieved by first adding about 2 tablespoons of milk per egg to the basic mix, only stirring the mixture about every 10 seconds or so while cooking and by taking the eggs off the heat about 1 minute before they are completely cooked, as the heat of the saucepan will continue cooking the eggs off the heat.

You will need:
15 g ($^{1}/_{2}$ oz) butter
4–6 small cherry tomatoes, halved (optional)
salt and freshly ground black pepper
$^{1}/_{2}$ teaspoon chopped chives
2 large eggs
4 tablespoons milk

To serve:
1 piece of buttered toast

1   Put half the butter into a saucepan. When hot, add the tomatoes and fry gently to soften somewhat, about 2 minutes. Season with salt and pepper and add the chopped chives. Remove from the pan and keep warm.
2   The same saucepan can be used for the eggs, though if a pure creamy scrambled egg is required, use a clean one. Whisk the eggs and milk together well, though without making them too frothy, and season with salt and pepper. Melt the remaining butter in the saucepan. When good and hot, add the egg mixture and stir gently about every 10 seconds (not constantly). When almost set, remove from the heat and stir until they're just right. Serve immediately with the hot buttered toast and tomatoes.

How to Boil the Perfect Egg

'They can't even boil an egg' is the ultimate put-down to describe someone's cooking skills. But boiling an egg properly isn't actually that simple. For a start, a good boiled egg is not boiled at all – it is simmered gently.

When first married, we had many 'discussions' regarding how to boil eggs. My husband cooked them straight from the fridge for three minutes in boiling water, so three minutes wasn't enough, and when the cold egg was immersed in the boiling water, the egg shell invariably cracked, allowing bits of egg white to hang out.

Always use really fresh eggs, preferably free range. A fresh egg will sink in a bowl of cold water, whereas older ones will float, as some of the liquid inside will have evaporated through the porous shell. (Because the shells are porous, eggs should never be stored beside strong-flavoured food like onions.)

Eggs – nature's convenience food – are nutritious for all age groups. They are rich in protein and easy-to-digest fat and contain many vitamins and minerals. They're also ideal for those watching their weight, as each egg contains only 80–90 calories, depending on its size.

There are two methods for boiling an egg, depending on whether it's come straight from the fridge or is at room temperature.

Suggested timings are given as a guide only, as saucepans and cookers vary.

Method 1: Fridge-cold eggs

Place the eggs in cold water in a saucepan, covering them completely. The moment the water comes to the boil, turn the heat down to a simmer and start timing the cooking.

- For a soft-boiled egg (medium or large egg), simmer for 3 minutes.
- For a hard white and a soft yolk (medium or large egg), simmer for 4 minutes.
- For hardboiled eggs (medium or large egg), simmer for 10 minutes.

Method 2: Room-temperature eggs

Bring a pot of water to a simmer. Add the eggs to the hot water, covering them completely. When the water returns to the same simmering point, start timing.

- For soft-boiled eggs (medium or large egg), simmer for 3–4 minutes.
- For a hard white and soft yolk (medium or large egg), simmer for 7 minutes.
- For hardboiled eggs (medium to large egg), simmer for 12 minutes.

NOTE: If serving hardboiled eggs cold in a salad, you can prevent an unattractive (but harmless) dark ring from appearing between the white and the yolk. To do this, crack the eggshells as soon as the eggs are cooked and plunge the whole egg into cold water to cool it as quickly as possible, then remove the shell completely.

French Mushroom Omelette

Serves 2

Unlike a Spanish tortilla (omelette), which is thick and cut into wedges, a French omelette is thin, with wrinkles in it. In this recipe, some mushrooms are first cooked until tasty in a little butter, cooled and added into the raw omelette mixture, which is then fried. Delicious.

NOTE: The size of the pan is relevant – if it's too large, the egg mixture will spread out too far and will be like a thin pancake with no delicious wrinkles.

NOTE: You can make two individual omelettes by dividing the mixture in half and using a 20.5 cm (8 inch) pan or make one large omelette in a 28 cm (11 inch) pan and cut the omelette in half when it's cooked.

You will need:
40 g (1¹/₂ oz) butter
2 tablespoons olive oil
1 shallot, finely chopped, or 1 tablespoon finely chopped onion
¹/₂ clove of garlic, finely chopped (or a bit more if liked)
125 g (generous 4 oz) mushrooms, finely chopped
salt and freshly ground black pepper
3–4 large eggs
1–2 tablespoons finely chopped fresh parsley
50 g (2 oz) cream cheese seasoned with a little salt and pepper (optional)

1   Melt half the butter in a frying pan with half the olive oil. Fry the shallot and garlic until soft, without browning. Add in the mushrooms and cook until soft and any liquid has evaporated, 3–5 minutes. Season to taste with salt and pepper, then spoon out onto a plate to cool quickly.
2   Put the eggs in a bowl and whisk with a fork to mix the yolks and the whites to an even texture, but try not to make them frothy. Add in salt and pepper, the parsley and the cooled mushroom mixture.
3   Heat the remaining butter and oil in the pan. When nice and hot, pour in the egg mixture. As soon as a thin layer at the base of the omelette sets in the pan, use a fork or spatula to draw the cooked egg in from the edge of the pan towards the centre of the omelette, which makes it wrinkle like fabric. Do this in a few places, letting the unset liquid egg mixture on top run out and cover the empty gap left on the pan (tilt the pan if necessary). When the bottom is golden and the top still nicely moist, remove the pan from the heat before the top is completely dried out, as it will continue to cook in its own heat.

4 Spread the cream cheese (if using) down the centre of the omelette and fold it in three. Tip out of the pan onto a warm plate.

Spicy Spinach Egg Nest

Serves 1

This is a meal in a pan in a jiffy. Garam masala is a standard mix of aromatic spices such as cinnamon, cloves and cardamom. The ingredients listed below make a generous meal for one, but if serving two, increase the ingredients by about half, with an extra egg or two. If preferred, the top of the eggs can be cooked by spooning some of the hot juices from the pan over them or by cooking under the grill.

You will need:

175 g (6 oz) fresh spinach

1 tablespoon olive oil

1 small onion, finely chopped

1 clove of garlic, crushed

50 g (2 oz) mushrooms, chopped

1 teaspoon garam masala

2 tomatoes, roughly chopped

salt and freshly ground black pepper

1–2 large eggs

50 g (2 oz) feta cheese

To serve:

crusty bread

1 Wash the spinach. If the leaves are large, tear them in half, discarding any strong stalks. Don't shake the excess water off the leaves after washing.

2 Heat the oil in a frying pan and cook the onion and garlic for 1–2 minutes, then add the mushrooms and fry for another few minutes, until soft. Stir in the garam masala. Add the tomatoes, season with salt and pepper and cook for 1–2 minutes. Pile in the spinach – it will look like too much, but it wilts right down in the heat. Cover with a lid and cook for 2–3 minutes, until the spinach softens.

3 Gently mix the contents of the pan together, then make a shallow well for each egg. Crack the eggs into the wells. Lightly season the top of each egg, adding a dribble of oil. Scatter the feta cheese around.

4 Cover the pan loosely with foil to allow the eggs to heat through, then remove the foil and cook under a hot grill for a couple of minutes to finish them off. Slide out onto a warm plate and serve immediately with crusty bread.

Smoked Haddock and Leek Quiche, page 20

Quiche

I LOVE THE sheer versatility of quiche. Serve it for lunch, brunch, picnics or anytime you fancy. Quiche, the savoury tart from Alsace that has swept the world, wasn't well known outside France until after the Second World War. Since then, it has spread to every wine bar and café. The authentic quiche Lorraine consists of a pastry base filled with a savoury egg and cream custard plus a small amount of cooked smoked bacon. Many wonderful variations have grown from this basic recipe.

The traditional French way of cooking a quiche is to first bake the empty pastry case. The pastry case is then filled with the egg and cream custard (and any other filling ingredients being used). It's then baked again, but this time at a lower temperature, which allows the custard to stay nice and moist.

Leftover slices of quiche can be frozen quite successfully. Simply allow them to thaw naturally rather than in a microwave, which seems to crumble up the pastry.

Baking a Pastry Case Blind

Baking 'blind' means baking an empty pastry case. A pastry case can be partly cooked before filling it and baking it again. This is to ensure that it's completely cooked underneath the filling. If the filling itself doesn't need to be cooked, the pastry case should be fully cooked, which may take a few minutes longer.

Pastry is a tricky son-of-a-gun since it can shrink like crazy in the oven. Never stretch the pastry to fit the tin – ease it in, otherwise it will shrink.

If making the pastry yourself, ensure the correct measurements are used. Also take care to use the minimum amount of liquid to bind the dry ingredients together, pressing the mixture with a fork to ensure it is squeezed thoroughly through.

When trimming the pastry around the edges of the tin, leave a small overhang to allow for shrinkage. A scissors is the perfect tool for this trimming job. Keep the trimmings just in case any holes should appear in the baked pastry case and some patchwork is required after baking. Applying the dough with some beaten egg will stick the patch in place to prevent leakage.

The pastry should be rested in the fridge for 15 minutes or so, then rolled out to line the tin.

Put the pastry-lined tin into the fridge, or better still, into the ice box or freezer, for another 15 minutes before baking. The pastry case can be quite chilled going into the oven – it will take a little longer to cook, but it keeps its shape very well during cooking.

To Bake Blind

Place a large piece of baking parchment in the chilled pastry case, large enough to run well up the sides. Spread a layer of dried beans or rice over the parchment. This keeps the pastry in place during baking. Bake in an oven preheated to 200°C/400°F/gas 6 for 10–12 minutes. Take out of the oven, remove the paper and beans and return to the oven and bake for a further 2–5 minutes to dry the base.

NOTE: I'VE MADE MANY TASTY QUICHES BY PUTTING THE FILLING INTO THE RAW PASTRY BASE AND BAKING THEM BOTH TOGETHER, ESPECIALLY IF I USE WHOLEMEAL PASTRY, WHICH BAKES NICE AND CRISPY ANYWAY. THE QUICHE WILL JUST NEED TO BE BAKED AT A HIGHER OVEN TEMPERATURE TO ENSURE THE PASTRY IS COOKED.

NOTE: IF YOU WISH TO PREPARE A QUICHE THE DAY BEFORE, THE PASTRY CASE CAN BE BAKED AND THE FILLING PREPARED, BUT DO NOT ASSEMBLE THE QUICHE UNTIL JUST BEFORE BAKING.

My Family Quiche

Serves 5

Frozen shortcrust pastry can be used, but for a special treat, make this tasty Parmesan pastry.

You will need:

For the pastry:

165 g (5³/₄ oz) white flour (not self-raising)

I rounded tablespoon ground almonds

I rounded tablespoon finely grated Parmesan cheese

salt and freshly ground black pepper

75 g (3 oz) chilled butter, cubed

3–5 tablespoons water

For the filling:

175 g (6 oz) rashers

1 onion, thinly sliced

1 clove of garlic, chopped

2–3 tablespoons olive oil

150 g (5 oz) mushrooms, chopped

salt and freshly ground black pepper

3–4 tomatoes, sliced

3 large eggs

225 ml (8 fl oz) cream, milk or a mixture of half and half

$^1/_2$ teaspoon mustard

40 g (1$^1/_2$ oz) grated mature cheddar cheese

1 tablespoon freshly grated Parmesan cheese (optional)

To serve:

green salad

You will also need a 24 cm (9$^1/_2$ inch) sandwich tin or fluted flan tin with a removable base. The tin should be at least 3.5 cm (1$^1/_4$ inches) deep.

1 **To make the pastry,** mix together the flour, ground almonds, Parmesan, salt and pepper. Rub in the cubes of butter until the mixture resembles breadcrumbs. This can be done quickly in a food processor (then transfer the mixture back into the bowl). Add just enough water to bind the dry ingredients together.

2 Using your hands, draw the pastry into one lump, kneading lightly, then cover with clingfilm and put into the fridge to rest for 15 minutes while you prepare the filling.

3 Once the pastry has been chilled, roll it out large enough to fit the base and sides of the tin. Lift the pastry with the rolling pin and lay it over the tin, easing it in to fit the tin (don't stretch the pastry, as this will make it shrink when cooking). Trim the edges, leaving a small overhang to allow for shrinkage. If you wish to bake the pastry case blind, see the directions on p.15. Otherwise put the following filling ingredients directly into the raw pastry case.

4 **To make the filling,** preheat the oven to 200°C/400°F/gas 6 if using a raw pastry case or 180°C/350°F/gas 4 if the pastry case is already cooked.

5 Grill the rashers and cut into bite-sized pieces. Fry the onion and garlic in some of the olive oil until soft. Lift out and set aside. Fry the mushrooms for a few minutes, until soft. Season with salt and pepper.

6 Spread the onion over the base of the pastry, top with the mushrooms and then scatter the rashers over. Arrange the tomatoes in a single layer over the lot.

7 Whisk together the eggs, cream and mustard and season with salt and pepper. Pour this over the filling – it should come up to the top. Sprinkle the grated cheeses over the top.

8 Bake for about 35 minutes, until the filling is set and golden brown and the pastry is cooked right through (allow an extra 15 minutes cooking time if the pastry was raw). Leave to stand in the tin for about 10 minutes before serving. Serve with a green salad and perhaps a glass of wine.

Bumper Leek, Spinach and Feta Quiche

Serves 8

The wholemeal flour gives this pastry a slight crunch, which makes a wonderful contrast to the delicious filling of dark green spinach and white, salty feta cheese, baked in the egg and cream custard. You can use cooked fresh spinach or frozen leaf spinach (thawed).

Using a large loose-bottomed flan tin 29 cm (11½ inches) in diameter and 4 cm (1½ inches) deep makes 8 generous servings.

You will need:

For the pastry:

150 g (5 oz) white flour

110 g (4 oz) wholemeal flour

salt and freshly ground black pepper

110 g (4 oz) chilled butter, cubed

4–7 tablespoons water

For the filling:

225 g (8 oz) thinly sliced leeks, washed well

1 clove of garlic, chopped

1–2 tablespoons olive oil

350–450 g (12–16 oz) frozen spinach (thawed)

salt and freshly ground black pepper

generous pinch of grated nutmeg

200 g (7 oz) feta cheese, coarsely crumbled

6 large eggs

250 (9 fl oz) cream (or a mixture of half milk, half cream)

1 teaspoon French mustard

To serve:

tomato salad

1 **To make the pastry,** mix the two flours and season with salt and pepper. Rub the butter into the flour until the mixture resembles breadcrumbs. This can be done quickly in a food processor (then transfer the mixture back into the bowl). Add the water, using a fork to mix the water through, squeezing well to use as little as possible to hold the dry ingredients together.

2 Using your hands, draw the pastry into one lump, kneading lightly. (Do not chill this pastry before rolling. It will get too stiff and will crack when rolled out.) Dust a board with wholemeal flour and roll the pastry out large enough to fit the base and sides of the tin. Lift the pastry with the rolling pin and lay it over the tin, easing it in to fit the tin (don't stretch the pastry, as this will make it shrink when cooking). Trim the edges, leaving a small overhang to allow for shrinkage. Chill in the fridge or freezer while you prepare the filling. Bake blind if wished (see p.15).

3 **To make the filling,** preheat the oven to 200°C/400°F/gas 6 if using a raw pastry case or to 180°C/350°F/gas 4 if the pastry case is already cooked.

4 Fry the leeks and garlic in the oil for 5–10 minutes, until soft. Arrange the leeks in a layer over the base of the pastry.

5 Drain any excess liquid off the thawed lumps of spinach, then season with salt, pepper and a pinch of nutmeg. Place the spinach in small clumps over the leeks. Scatter the crumbled feta cheese evenly around the spinach.

6 Whisk together the eggs, cream and mustard and season with salt and pepper. Pour the egg mixture over the filling – it should reach the top of the filling.

7 Bake for 45 minutes, or until the filling is set, the pastry is cooked right through and the top is golden. Serve with a tomato salad.

Smoked Haddock and Leek Quiche

See photograph, page 14

Serves 6

Smoking is an ancient preservation technique, which is actually a kind of slow, low-temperature cooking. It's also a chemical treatment – smoke is a complex material with upwards of 200 components, some of which partly preserve and flavour the food. Nowadays, however, smoking white fish, such as cod and haddock, is done more as a flavouring and colouring method than as a way of preserving the fish, so the fish has to be cooked before eating.

Much of the smoked cod and haddock available in Ireland has been dyed with a bright orange colour. If you have time, search for naturally smoked fillets. They are a much paler colour, a cross between creamy beige and light tan. The difference in flavour will make your search worthwhile. Don't leave the fish sitting in your fridge – use it as soon as possible.

Smoked salmon, smoked mackerel and smoked trout are different. These have been smoked in such a way that they are ready to eat and require no cooking. They are usually sold in vacuum packs. Check the use-by dates on the packets: once opened the fish should be consumed within 2–3 days.

Choose the thickest part of the fillet of smoked haddock, as it breaks into more meaty flakes.

You will need:

For the rich shortcrust pastry:

175 g (6 oz) plain flour

100 g (3¹/₂ oz) chilled butter, cubed

salt and freshly ground black pepper

5 tablespoons water (or more if required)

For the filling:

25 g (1 oz) butter

¹/₂ tablespoon olive oil

225 g (8 oz) thinly sliced leeks, washed well

salt and freshly ground black pepper

350 g (12 oz) smoked haddock

small bunch of chives

3 large eggs

1 x 250 ml carton (9 fl oz) cream

¹/₂ teaspoon French mustard

3 tablespoon finely grated Parmesan (optional)

To serve:

green salad

1 **To make the pastry,** preheat the oven to heat to 200°C/400°F/gas 6.

2 Put the flour, butter and seasoning into a food processor and buzz together for seconds at a time, until the mixture looks like fine breadcrumbs. Turn into a bowl and stir in just enough water to bind the ingredients together. Press firmly through until the mixture comes together into a lump. Knead briefly until fairly smooth (I usually do this in the bowl). Cover the pastry and allow it to rest for 20 minutes in the fridge, then roll out thinly on a floured surface to a round large enough to fit into a 25 cm (9 ½ inch) loose-bottomed flan tin about 4 cm (1½ inches) deep. Chill again in the ice box or freezer for about 20 minutes. Remove the pastry-lined tin from the fridge and bake blind (see p.15).

3 **Meanwhile, to make the filling,** lower the oven temperature to 190°C/375°F/gas 5 once the pastry case is done.

4 Melt the butter in a large pan, add the oil and the leeks and some seasoning and cook gently, uncovered, for 5–10 minutes, stirring occasionally, until tender.

5 Boil some water in a large shallow pan (a frying pan will do). Add the haddock and simmer for about 4 minutes, until just cooked. Lift out onto a plate and leave until cool enough to handle, then break the fish into large flakes, discarding any skin and bones.

6 Using a scissors, snip the chopped chives into the leeks, then scatter the leeks over the base of the pastry case. Scatter the flaked fish over the top of the leeks.

7 Beat the eggs with the cream, mustard and Parmesan and season with salt and pepper, then pour over the leeks and fish. Bake for 30–35 minutes, until just set and lightly browned on top. Remove from the oven and leave to stand for about 10 minutes before serving. Serve with a green salad.

Variations

SMOKED SALMON AND LEEK QUICHE

Use the recipe above, omitting the smoked haddock and using about 200 g (7 oz) of smoked salmon instead. When placing the smoked salmon in the pastry case on top of the layer of leeks, arrange the slices in such a way that they are draped in 'waves' rather than laid flat.

HAM AND LEEK QUICHE

Use the recipe above, omitting the smoked haddock and using 350 g (12 oz) chopped home-cooked ham instead.

CHAPTER 2

Starters and Finger Food

IN 1817, THE PRINCE REGENT gave a dinner party at the Brighton Pavilion that began with four different kinds of soup and proceeded via a fish stew to trout, turbot and eel on to ham, goose, truffled chicken and veal. These were followed by 36 entrées, which included salmon, partridges and sirloin of beef. As if that weren't enough, there followed eight pastry reproductions of famous buildings, then roast goose and partridge. Close behind came lobsters, oysters, cakes and soufflés – about 100 courses in all.

Mercifully, our version of a good meal can start with something small, tasty and not too difficult to prepare. I like to call this course 'sitting down food'. The main task of a starter course is to get everyone settled and prepared for the more substantial course to follow. Finger food suitable for passing around with drinks can also take the place of a starter for a less formal meal.

A good tapas bar is like an Aladdin's cave, with all manner of foods and dishes on display to choose from. Tapas can be as simple as a little dish of olives, a few slices of mature Manchego cheese or some Serrano ham. There is also a large range of cooked dishes to choose from that are served in small tapas portions, or one can choose to have a racion, that is, a meal-sized portion of your favourite dish.

Pinchos are a form of tapas that are native to the Basque country in northern Spain. These snacks are traditionally served on small pieces of bread and arranged on platters which customers help themselves from. They can be rough and ready or a little more delicate. Pinchos make ideal finger food to serve before a meal or with drinks.

FROM BRENDA'S KITCHEN

Pinchos with Artichokes and Cream Cheese

Makes 12

For these pinchos, choose a thin baton of French bread or a narrow bread roll so the slices aren't too big and so that the sliced tinned artichokes fit neatly on top.

You will need:
12 small circular slices of French bread
butter
cream cheese (or cream cheese with chives), to spread
6 tinned artichoke hearts, drained
6 green olives (the kind stuffed with red pimiento), halved
a few fresh thyme leaves
freshly ground black pepper

1 Toast the bread and immediately spread with a smidgen of butter to prevent the toast from drying out and becoming too hard. When cold, generously spread each slice with the cream cheese.
2 Using a very sharp knife, cut two slices off the top of each artichoke heart, taking care to keep the circular shape intact. (The remaining pieces of artichoke can be used in a salad.) Sit a slice of the artichoke on each circle of cream cheese, then place a halved olive in the centre of each.
3 Scatter lightly with the fresh thyme leaves and a little freshly ground black pepper.

Mushroom Pinchos with Cashel Blue

See photograph, page 24

Makes 12

Choose small button mushrooms and pull out the stalk to make a little cup. Fill with a simple stuffing and top with Cashel blue cheese. Bake in the oven until the cheese melts. These can be prepared in advance and baked shortly before serving. I have served these on their own, but they can also be served on small circles of lightly buttered toast (use a small scone cutter to cut out neat circles of toast).

> **You will need:**
> **12 button mushrooms, stalks removed**
> **1–2 tablespoons olive oil**
> **1 tablespoon finely chopped onion**
> **$^1/_2$ small clove of garlic, chopped**
> **1–2 heaped tablespoons fresh breadcrumbs**
> **a few pinches of herbes de Provence or oregano**
> **$^1/_2$ teaspoon finely grated lemon zest**
> **1–2 teaspoons lemon juice**
> **salt and freshly ground black pepper**
> **12 tiny slices of Cashel blue cheese to fit on top of the mushrooms**

1 Preheat the oven to 190°C/375°F/gas 5. Line the base of a baking tin with tinfoil and brush lightly with olive oil.

2 Cut a small piece off the rounded side of each mushroom so that the mushroom cups will sit flat, then place on the foil-lined tin. Drizzle a little olive oil into each cup. Fry the onion and garlic in a little olive oil to soften them, then add in the breadcrumbs, herbs and the lemon zest and juice. Season to taste.

3 Divide the breadcrumb mixture between the mushrooms and place a piece of blue cheese on top of each one. Cover very loosely with a piece of oiled foil (so it won't stick to the cheese). Bake for about 5 minutes, then remove the foil. Bake for a further 5 minutes, or until the cheese has melted and the mushrooms are tender. If too much of the cheese has oozed onto the foil, scoop it back up on top again while still piping hot. Serve these pinchos while they're still warm.

Spicy Melon with Serrano Ham

See photograph, page 24

Makes 12–16

The flavour of Serrano ham goes perfectly with melon (Parma ham could also be used). However, I find the stringy bits in the ham are quite tough to chew without the use of a knife and fork to cut them up, so when serving as finger food, I make sure to cut the Serrano ham into short chewable lengths. A scissors is a handy tool for this job.

You will need:

12–16 bite-sized chunks of melon (about half a small Galia or Ogen melon)

paprika or hot paprika, to dust

6–8 thin slices of vacuum-packed Serrano ham

cocktail sticks

1 Dust the chunks of melon with a little of the paprika. Cut the slices of ham into narrow strips. Gather a generous bite of ham on each cocktail stick and stick into the melon chunks.

Salted Almond Nibbles

See photograph, page 24

Serves 3–6

Native to Spain, these almonds are fried until golden in olive oil.

You will need:

200g (7 oz) whole blanched almonds

1–2 tablespoons olive oil

salt

1 Heat a thin layer of oil in a pan and fry the almonds until golden. They will be slow to turn golden brown at first, but when they do they will get too brown very quickly, so take care they don't burn. Lift out onto kitchen paper and shake salt generously over. Allow to cool completely.

Salmon Bites

See photograph, page 34

Makes about 10 cubes

These are simply thick, skinless salmon fillets cut into little cubes and fried, then served with a little sweet chilli sauce drizzled on top. These are best served fresh, but they can be fried in advance and reheated in a moderate oven for 5–10 minutes.

You will need:

200g (7 oz) skinless salmon fillet (choose one that is a nice even thickness)

a little olive oil to fry

salt and freshly ground black pepper

a few teaspoons of sweet chilli sauce (available in shops)

cocktail sticks

To serve:

extra sweet chilli sauce for dipping

1 Cut the salmon into small cubes. Fry in the olive oil until golden on each side (3–5 minutes), by which time they should be cooked through. Season lightly with salt and pepper. Pierce a cocktail stick into each cube and spoon a little of the chilli sauce over each one. If liked, serve extra chilli sauce in a tiny bowl for dipping.

Tiger Prawns on Cucumber Slices

Makes 18–20

Buy the prawns already cooked, then marinate them for extra flavour.

You will need:

18–20 cooked tiger prawns (choose a good size)

1–2 tablespoons olive oil

¹/₂–1 tablespoon lemon juice

small sliver of garlic

salt and freshly ground black pepper

pinch of cayenne pepper

mayonnaise

18–20 slices of cucumber (not too thin)

18–20 cocktail sticks

1   Thaw the prawns if necessary.
2   Put the oil, lemon juice, garlic, salt, pepper and cayenne pepper in a saucepan. Gently heat together for 1–2 minutes and then allow to cool. When cold, add the prawns and leave to marinate in the fridge for 1 hour or longer.
3   Put a little dollop of mayonnaise on each slice of cucumber. Drain the prawns. Pierce a cocktail stick through each prawn and place in an upright position into each cucumber slice.

Mini Crab Cakes on Cracked Poppadoms

Makes 20–24 small cakes

These can be made in advance and reheated just before serving.

You will need:
175 g (6 oz) fresh crabmeat, brown and white
salt and freshly ground black pepper
I small egg, beaten lightly
I tablespoon mayonnaise
I–2 teaspoons Dijon mustard
I tablespoon finely chopped fresh parsley
I teaspoon finely grated lemon zest
2–4 spring onions, finely chopped
25–50 g (1–2 oz) fine breadcrumbs
oil, for frying
4–6 poppadoms

1   Place the crab in a bowl and season with salt and pepper. If the crabmeat appears rather moist, squeeze out the excess moisture or the cakes will be too soft. Add the egg, mayonnaise, mustard, parsley, lemon zest and spring onions. Mix and add just enough breadcrumbs to bind.
2   Heat some oil in a frying pan. When hot, spoon out the mixture in spoonfuls the size of a small walnut and fry the little cakes for 2 minutes on each side, until browned on both sides.
3   Cook the poppadoms, one at a time, in a microwave on high for about 1 minute each, or in hot oil. Just before serving, break into small pieces and put a crab cake on each one.

Crostini

The word crostini is derived from the Italian 'crosta' (crust). These make tasty starters or snacks for any time.

You will need:

4 slices of fat French bread, cut at a slant

a generous drizzle of fruity olive oil

salt and freshly ground black pepper

$\frac{1}{2}$ clove of garlic

1 Heat the oven to 190°C/375°F/gas 5 (or the crostini can be cooked under the grill if preferred).
2 Place the slices of French bread on a baking tin, drizzle generously with the olive oil and season lightly with salt and pepper. Bake for 10 minutes, until golden, or toast each side under the grill. Remove from the oven and rub the top of each bread slice with the cut piece of garlic.

Crostini with Prawns

Serves 3

A carton of tiger prawns cured in brine will work for this recipe, or use freshly cooked prawns.

You will need:

2 tablespoons extra virgin olive oil

25 g (1 oz) butter

1 clove of garlic, crushed

100 g (about 4 oz) prawns, brine drained off

1 tablespoon chopped chives

1 tablespoon chopped flat leaf parsley

salt and freshly ground black pepper

squeeze of lemon juice, to taste

3 crostini, prepared as above

1 Put the oil and butter into a pan and fry the garlic until soft. Add all the remaining ingredients. Spoon the mixture onto the crostini and serve warm.

Crostini with Chicken Livers

Serves 4

Fresh chicken livers have a delicious flavour when fried. Wholegrain mustard gives a tasty zing to the finished dish.

You will need:
225 g (8 oz) fresh chicken livers
15 g ($^1/_2$ oz) butter
1 tablespoon olive oil
1–2 tablespoons finely chopped onion
1 clove of garlic, chopped
$^1/_8$–$^1/_4$ teaspoon oregano
4–6 tablespoons crème fraîche or cream
1 teaspoon wholegrain mustard
4 crostini, prepared as on p. 31
chopped fresh chives, to garnish

To serve:
tossed salad (optional)

1 Put the chicken livers to soak in a bowl of cold water and steep for 10 minutes. Drain thoroughly and pat dry with paper towels.
2 Heat the butter and olive oil in a frying pan and gently fry the onion and garlic for 30–60 seconds, until soft. Add the chicken livers, seasoning them with salt and pepper and the oregano as they fry. After a few minutes, when they're nicely browned and just cooked through, add the crème fraîche or cream and the mustard and cook together to heat through.
3 To serve, place one crostini on each serving plate and spoon the chicken liver mixture onto each. Garnish with the chopped chives. If liked, accompany with a small serving of tossed salad.

Salmon Bites (above), page 28
Two-Salmon Rillettes on Crostini (below)

Two-Salmon Rillettes on Crostini

Makes 16

Fresh and smoked salmon combine to make a tasty topping for these crostini. Correctly speaking, rillettes is the French name for a type of potted pork – that is, pork that has been very well cooked so that it flakes to make a kind of coarse paste. In this recipe, the two salmons are flaked after cooking and mixed with all the ingredients that have been cooked in the pan.

You will need:

50 g (2 oz) butter

I teaspoon olive oil

I rounded tablespoon finely chopped shallot or onion

I small clove of garlic, crushed

275 g (10 oz) fresh salmon fillet, skinned and chopped

juice of ¹/₂ lemon

I tablespoon finely chopped fresh dill or parsley

salt and freshly ground black pepper

150 g (5 oz) smoked salmon, cut into medium-sized chunks

25 g (I oz) clarified butter (optional – see note)

16 crostini, prepared as on page 31

1   To make the salmon mixture, melt the butter with the oil in a frying pan and gently fry the onion and garlic for 1 minute, until soft. Add the fresh salmon and fry gently for 3–5 minutes, until cooked through. Add the lemon juice, dill, salt and pepper. Add the smoked salmon and heat gently until it's thoroughly heated through (it will change colour).

2   Using two forks, shred the fish into fine flakes and mix well. Transfer all the contents of the pan into a small dish and press down evenly. If you wish to keep this in the fridge for a few days, cover the top with a layer of clarified butter to seal in the freshness.

3   To serve, scrape back the covering of clarified butter (if used) and put small spoonfuls of the salmon mixture in neat mounds on the crostini. Garnish with tiny sprigs of dill and arrange prettily on a serving plate.

NOTE: THE OBJECT OF CLARIFYING BUTTER IS TO REMOVE THE MILK SOLIDS AND THE SALT IN THE BUTTER, THUS OBTAINING A CLEAR FAT. TO CLARIFY BUTTER, MELT 40G (1¹/₂ OZ) BUTTER IN A LITTLE SAUCEPAN UNTIL A GOOD FOAM COMES TO THE TOP. TAKE OFF THE HEAT AND ALLOW TO STAND FOR I MINUTE OR SO. SKIM OFF ANY FROTH THAT HAS FLOATED TO THE TOP AND POUR GENTLY INTO A CLEAN DISH OR JAR SO THAT ONLY THE CLEAR FAT POURS OFF, LEAVING ANY MILKY SEDIMENT BEHIND TO BE DISCARDED.

Crusty Goat's Cheese with Beetroot Jam

Serves 3–4

Choose a round, log-shaped cheese that can be sliced. The size of the slices will determine whether you need one or two per serving. Dipped in egg and breadcrumbs and lightly fried, the slices of goat's cheese are served hot with a tossed salad and some beetroot jam, which complements the flavour of the cheese.

You will need:

200 g (7 oz) goat's cheese (log shaped)

flour, to dust

1 large egg, beaten

salt and freshly ground black pepper

75 g (3 oz) fine breadcrumbs
  (preferably toasted)

oil for frying (vegetable or olive)

To serve:

beetroot jam (see below)

salad with honey mustard dressing (see
  below)

NOTE: Dipping a sharp knife in boiling water helps to cut the cheese cleanly.

1   If the log of goat's cheese has a thin rind on it, leave it on except at the front and back end – cut this off very thinly and discard.
2   Cut the goat's cheese into circular slices and dust each circle lightly with flour, brushing off the excess. Season the beaten egg with salt and pepper. Place the breadcrumbs in a flat dish and season with salt and pepper.
3   Dip the slices of cheese one at a time into the beaten egg, allowing the excess to drip off, then place in the breadcrumbs, pressing firmly to coat well. Heat some oil in a frying pan and fry the prepared slices on both sides until golden, making sure the edges of the slices are golden too. If necessary, you may need to hold the slices on their side (using a tongs) in order to brown the edges. Serve with the tossed salad and a generous spoonful of the beetroot jam.

Beetroot Jam

Do not use pickled beetroot to make the jam, but rather the ready-cooked beets available in vacuum packs.

You will need:

2 cooked beetroots (from a vacuum pack)

1–2 spoons of blackcurrant jam, to taste

I Put the beetroot and jam into a food processor and buzz until the beetroot is reduced to quite small dice. If no processor is available, simply chop the beetroot finely and then mash with the jam. The beetroot will not become a creamy purée, but rather will be grainy.

Salad with Honey and Mustard Dressing

You will need:

I packet baby leaf salad

4 tablespoons olive oil

I tablespoon fresh lemon juice or balsamic vinegar

I teaspoon runny honey

$^{1}/_{2}$ teaspoon wholegrain mustard

salt and freshly ground black pepper

I Mix all the dressing ingredients together. When ready to serve, simply toss well with the baby salad leaves.

NOTE: IF YOU ARE MADE A FREEMAN OF THE CITY OF DUBLIN, ONE OF THE PERKS YOU'RE ENTITLED TO IS TO GRAZE A GOAT IN ST STEPHEN'S GREEN. THE PRODUCTION OF GOAT'S CHEESE, ONCE A VERY FRENCH THING, IS NOW FAIRLY COMMON IN IRELAND.

Pear and Goat's Cheese Pastry Puffs

Serves 6

A delightful starter for a meal, these are easy to prepare and serve. Little circles of ready-made puff pastry are spread with cranberry sauce, then topped with wedges of pears, sliced goat's cheese and toasted walnuts. These can be prepared in advance and popped into the oven 15 minutes before required.

You will need:

3 pears

40 g (1¹/₂oz) butter

1 generous tablespoon brown sugar

1 roll from a packet of ready-rolled puff pastry

2 tablespoons cranberry sauce

125 g (4¹/₂ oz) goat's cheese

a little melted butter (optional)

50 g (2 oz) chopped walnuts or hazelnuts, toasted

To serve:

6 small handfuls baby leaf salad with honey and mustard dressing (see p.37)

1 Preheat the oven to 200°C/400°F/gas 6.
2 Peel the pears and cut into narrow wedges, discarding the cores. Melt the butter in a pan, add the brown sugar and cook gently until the sugar has melted. Add the pears and cook gently for a few minutes, until they are well flavoured by the sugar mixture but still keep their shape – do not allow them to become mushy.
3 Unroll the pastry. Using a large cutter (minimum of 9 cm/3¹/₂ inches diameter), or a small upturned bowl, cut out 6 circles and place them on a baking sheet. Spread 1 teaspoon of cranberry sauce in the centre of each pastry circle. Place 2–3 pieces of pear on each pastry circle, then place a small circle of goat's cheese on the pastry beside the pears (or slightly overlapping). If the slices are too large, cut into halves or quarters. Drizzle some of the melted butter over the cheese to help it brown, then scatter a teaspoon or so of the nuts over each circle.
4 15 minutes before serving, put the pastry circles into the hot oven. Bake for 15 minutes, or until the pastry is well puffed up and the cheese is melted. Serve at once, placing each pastry on a small serving plate with some tossed salad on the side.

NOTE: IF PREPARING IN ADVANCE, ALLOW THE PEARS TO GET COLD BEFORE PUTTING THEM ON TOP OF THE PASTRY.

Twice-Baked Two-Cheese Soufflés

Serves 5–6 as a starter

These individual soufflés will collapse when removed from the oven after baking, but it doesn't matter! Just before serving, the once-baked soufflés are turned out upside down onto an ovenproof serving plate. Some cream is spooned over them, they are popped back into the oven and they puff up a little on this second baking.

Two types of cheese give greater flavour to this recipe. I like to use a mature cheddar like Wexford or Kilmeaden. Some grated Parmesan adds even more flavour. Needless to say, Parmesan that you grate fresh yourself has a much better flavour than the ready-grated variety.

These savoury soufflés are suitable to serve as starters or as light lunch dishes. If serving as a lunch dish, be more generous with the quantities.

NOTE: IT'S WORTH NOTING THAT AFTER THE FIRST BAKING, THESE SOUFFLÉS WILL COLLAPSE BACK DOWN TO APPROXIMATELY THE SAME SIZE THEY WERE BEFORE BAKING. THEREFORE, YOU CAN ADJUST THE QUANTITIES YOU USE AS YOU SEE FIT.

You will need:

50 g (2 oz) butter

50 g (2 oz) flour

300 ml ($\frac{1}{2}$ pint) milk

75 g (3 oz) grated mature cheddar cheese, plus extra for the second baking

1–2 tablespoons grated Parmesan cheese, plus extra for the second baking

1 scant teaspoon French mustard

salt and freshly ground black pepper

3 large eggs, separated

150 ml (5 fl oz) cream

To serve:

chives and curls of freshly grated Parmesan cheese

1 Preheat the oven to 190°C/375°F/gas 5. Grease 6 individual ramekins (approximately 150 ml–175 ml/5–6 fl oz in size). Place a circle of baking parchment in the base of each one.
2 Put the butter, flour and milk into a saucepan. Using a whisk, stir briskly over a moderate heat until everything melts. Change to a wooden spoon and, stirring constantly, bring to

the boil. The sauce will be very thick. Allow to cook for a few seconds, stirring very fast to prevent any suggestion of it getting burned at the bottom. Take off the heat and add the cheeses, mustard and seasoning. When partly cooled, beat in the egg yolks.

3　Beat the egg whites in a separate bowl until stiff. Add one-quarter of the beaten egg whites to the sauce mixture and stir thoroughly. Gently fold in all the remaining egg whites.

4　Divide the mixture between the prepared ramekins and stand the filled dishes in a roasting tin. Pour in enough warm water to come about halfway up the sides of the ramekins.

5　Bake for about 15-20 minutes, or until puffed up and golden. Remove from the oven and leave in their dishes until ready to serve. (The soufflés can be frozen at this stage.) Reduce the oven temperature to 180°C/350°F/gas 4.

6　To serve, turn the soufflés out onto individual ovenproof plates (or one large one) and peel off the parchment paper to reveal a smooth base. Spoon 2 tablespoons of cream over each soufflé, then sprinkle a little of each of the grated cheeses on top and season lightly with salt and pepper. Bake for about 12 minutes, until the soufflés have heated through and turned light golden in spots. The soufflés will also puff up very slightly.

7　Serve immediately, garnished with chives and curls of freshly grated Parmesan (these are easily cut off a wedge of Parmesan cheese with a vegetable peeler).

Variations:

To make twice-baked smoked salmon soufflés, omit the cheeses and the French mustard in the above recipe and use 100g (almost 4 oz) chopped smoked salmon (or smoked sea trout) instead, with 1 tablespoon lemon juice and a dash of English mustard. When baking for the second time, sprinkle with the cream and a little Parmesan cheese.

Prawn and Avocado Starter

Serves 4

This can be prepared a few hours in advance, as the vinegar in the dressing prevents the avocado from becoming discoloured. Ideally, put each serving in a ramekin, then turn out onto serving plates shortly before serving. The ingredients will hold the shape of the ramekin dish quite well.

Choose prawns in brine, as they have a good salty flavour that will contrast nicely with the avocado. Alternatively, the prawns can be substituted with smoked salmon (as shown in the photograph).

This was inspired by a recipe from Paul Rankin.

NOTE: TAKE CARE WHEN MIXING ALL THE INGREDIENTS TOGETHER — DON'T STIR TOO ROUGHLY, OTHERWISE THE AVOCADOS WILL LOSE THEIR SHAPE AND BECOME MUSHY.

You will need:
1 large avocado, ripe but not too ripe
honey mustard dressing (see p.37)
2 plum tomatoes or firm ripe tomatoes (175g/6 oz)
4 spring onions, chopped (choose thin ones)
110–150 g (4–5 oz) cooked prawns (or smoked salmon, chopped)
salt and freshly ground black or white pepper

To serve:
4 handfuls baby salad leaves
crusty bread

1 Cut the avocados in half, peel them and remove the stones, then dice the flesh. Immediately put into a bowl and add enough of the honey mustard dressing to coat generously.
2 Skin the tomatoes, cut them in half and discard the seeds. Dice the remaining flesh and put in a separate bowl. Add the spring onions and prawns or chopped smoked salmon. Season lightly with salt and pepper and a little of the dressing and mix well. Add the prepared avocados to the prawn or salmon mixture and gently mix everything together. Divide between the 4 ramekin dishes. Cover the dishes with cling film and chill until ready to serve.
3 To serve, remove the cling film, cover each ramekin with an upturned serving plate, then invert the two and gently lift off the ramekin. Toss the salad leaves in the rest of the honey mustard dressing and arrange a little at the side of each plate. Serve with crusty bread.

NOTE: To skin tomatoes, put them in a heatproof bowl and cover with boiling water. Leave them to stand for 60 seconds, or until the skins start to split. Immediately transfer to a bowl of cold water to cool quickly. The skins should now peel off quite easily using a sharp knife.

NOTE: To ripen avocados at home, put them in a brown paper bag with a banana for a couple of days.

CHAPTER 3

Soups

Soups are wonderfully versatile and satisfying, suitable for serving on so many different occasions. They're great as a starter, a snack or even as a main dish followed by a hearty dessert, and they are also good in picnic baskets. Soups make excellent family food, especially on weekends, when everyone seems to be coming and going to sports and other commitments. A pot of soup provides instant nourishment that can be reheated in a blink. There's nothing to beat homemade soup for goodness and flavour.

A good stock is important for most soups. Good-quality stock cubes make a successful stock when you are in a hurry, though sometimes it's worth the effort to make the real thing. Chicken stock is easily made if you are boiling a chicken for the main meal. (For example, see the recipe for chicken and chorizo pie on p.156.)

Soups actually benefit from being made a little in advance and then reheated, as this allows the flavours to mingle. Cover any leftovers and store in the fridge for a couple of days, or better still, freeze in single portions, ready for a quick snack.

There are two basic steps in making soup. One is to sauté (fry gently or 'sweat') the onions, garlic and vegetables in a little fat or oil, stirring occasionally, to soften and flavour them without changing colour. If any meat is being used, it also is usually sautéed at the start. The second step is to cook all the ingredients gently in stock until tender.

A third step is included for some soups, which is to purée the cooked vegetables using a blender, food processor or hand-held blender. If none of these is available, simply use a potato masher – either strain off the vegetables to mash them, or carefully mash in the saucepan itself.

NOTE: SAVE THE TASTY JUICES AND FAT LEFT IN THE TIN AFTER ROASTING A CHICKEN, AS THEY ADD GREAT FLAVOUR TO A SOUP. ANY REMAINING CHICKEN FAT FROM THE ROASTING TIN CAN BE USED INSTEAD OF OR IN CONJUNCTION WITH OIL OR BUTTER WHEN FRYING THE VEGETABLES IN THE PREPARATION OF SOME SOUPS.

NOTE: A HEAVY, WIDE SAUCEPAN WITH A LID IS IDEAL FOR MAKING SOUP, AS THIS ALLOWS FOR SLOW SIMMERING ON THE COOKER WITH A MINIMUM FEAR OF BURNING.

Cheese, Garlic and Herb Bread, page 257
Chunky Chicken Soup, page 49

Butternut Squash Soup

Serves 6 as a starter or 4 as a main lunch dish

The vibrant orange colour of the squash makes a wonderful soup, both to look at and to eat. A little freshly grated ginger gives a nice twist to the flavour. Serve with crispy garlic croutons (see p. 48) and some crème fraîche spooned on top of each serving to complete the flavour.

NOTE: BUTTERNUT SQUASH WILL KEEP FOR WEEKS IN A VEGETABLE RACK, PROVIDED IT'S DRY AND COOL.

You will need:

1 butternut squash (when diced, the flesh will weigh about 450–700 g/1–1 ¹/₂ lb)

50g (2 oz) butter

1 tablespoon olive oil

1 large onion, chopped

2 cloves of garlic, chopped (optional)

1 potato, peeled and diced

1 large carrot, peeled and diced small

2 sticks of celery, chopped

1 dessertspoon grated fresh ginger

1 teaspoon ground coriander

¹/₂ teaspoon ground cumin

salt and freshly ground black pepper

900 ml (1¹/₂ pints) vegetable or chicken stock

To serve:

crème fraîche or fromage frais

chopped fresh chives

garlic croutons (see p. 48)

1 Using a sharp knife, cut the butternut squash in half, scoop out the seeds and the fibrous matter around them and discard. Peel the squash, then dice it into pieces about 1 cm (¹/₂ inch) in size.

2 Melt the butter in a heavy-based saucepan with the olive oil. Gently cook the onion and garlic without browning for a few minutes, until soft. Add the potato, carrot and celery and stir over a gentle heat until they are well coated in the butter and oil. Add the grated ginger, coriander, cumin, salt and pepper and the stock. Bring to the boil, cover the saucepan with a lid and simmer gently for 20–30 minutes, until the vegetables are tender.

3 Serve with spoonfuls of crème fraîche or fromage frais on top of each serving and sprinkle with chopped chives. Serve with the crunchy garlic croutons on top or separately.

Garlic Croutons

Makes approximately 75 g (3 oz)

Packets of ready-made croutons are readily available, though it's very easy to make your own. Croutons can be fried in a pan or cooked in the oven, which uses less oil. Go ahead and make plenty of croutons, because they store well in a plastic bag or airtight container.

You will need:
4 slices of slightly stale bread, crusts removed
4 tablespoons olive oil
I clove of garlic
salt and pepper
herbes de Provence

Cut the bread into 1 cm ($^1/_2$ inch) cubes or smaller.

To fry: Heat the oil in a frying pan, add the garlic and cook gently for about 30 seconds to flavour the oil, then remove the garlic. Fry the cubes in a single layer in the pan, turning as required until golden all over. It may be necessary to add a bit more oil. Drain on paper kitchen towels and season with salt and pepper and pinches of dried herbes de Provence while still warm.

To cook in the oven: Preheat the oven to 180°C/350°F/gas 4. Spread 2–4 tablespoons of the oil on a baking tray, add the garlic and put into the oven to heat for a few minutes. Then add the cubes of bread, tossing them in the oil as best you can, or add a little more oil if you like. Remove the garlic, put the tin back into the oven and bake for about 10 minutes, or until the croutons are nice and crispy. Keep a sharp eye on them so they don't over-brown. Drain on paper kitchen towels and season with salt and pepper and pinches of dried herbes de Provence while still warm.

Chunky Chicken Soup

See photograph, page 45

Serves 4–6

This chunky soup, which is ideal for a light lunch dish, evolved when I was hungry and tired and had a few skinless chicken breasts in the fridge. Another bonus is that this reheats well. Serve with crusty bread and perhaps a little cheese.

You will need:

1 large onion, chopped

2 cloves of garlic, chopped

2–4 tablespoons olive oil

175 g (6 oz) mushrooms, chopped

salt and freshly ground black pepper

4 skinless chicken breast fillets, cut into chunks (about 6–8 chunks per fillet, depending on size)

2 medium potatoes, peeled and chopped

2 sticks celery, chopped finely

900 ml (1½ pints) water

1½–2 chicken stock cubes, crumbled

¼ teaspoon mixed herbs

1 bay leaf

300 ml (½ pint) milk

kneaded butter (see note)

1 tablespoon chopped fresh parsley or chives

NOTE: To make kneaded butter, mash together 1 tablespoon butter (or polyunsaturated margarine) and 1 tablespoon flour to make a paste.

1 Using a heavy-based saucepan, fry the onion and garlic in the olive oil for a few minutes, until soft. Add the mushrooms and fry for a further 3–4 minutes, until soft, adding a little more oil if necessary. Season with salt and pepper.

2 Fry the chicken chunks in two batches, until they turn white. Add the potatoes and celery to the saucepan along with the water, stock cubes, mixed herbs and bay leaf. Bring to the boil, cover with a lid and simmer gently for 20 minutes, until all the ingredients are tender.

3 Add the milk and drop in the kneaded butter, in small pieces, and bring the soup back to the boil. Using a whisk, stir briskly and constantly to mix in the kneaded butter until the soup thickens slightly. Add the parsley and continue to simmer briskly for about 1 minute or so to cook the paste. Taste for seasoning.

Moroccan Spiced Soup

Serves 5–6

There are lots of spices and vegetables in this soup, so this is comforting on a cold day – or any day. This 'meal-in-a-bowl' soup is based on a classic North African soup that's often served in the evening during the month of Ramadan, when Muslims fast from sun-up until sundown each day. I like to serve it with scoops of crème fraîche on each serving, accompanied by crusty bread or Indian naan bread. This soup reheats well.

You will need:

1 large onion, chopped

1 large clove of garlic, chopped

2 tablespoons olive oil

2 carrots, diced

2 celery sticks, diced

350 g (12 oz) potatoes, diced

1 teaspoon cinnamon

1 teaspoon turmeric (optional)

1 tablespoon finely grated fresh ginger

$^1/_8$–$^1/_4$ teaspoon cayenne pepper, to taste

salt and freshly ground black pepper

900 ml (1$^1/_2$ pints) vegetable stock

1 x 400 g (14 oz) tin chopped tomatoes

1 x 400 g (14 oz) tin chickpeas, drained

1–3 teaspoons sugar

2 tablespoons chopped fresh coriander

1 tablespoon lemon juice

To serve:

croutons

crème fraîche or Greek-style yoghurt

naan bread

1 In a heavy-based saucepan, fry the onion and garlic in the oil until soft but not coloured. Add the carrots, celery and potatoes. Add the spices to the vegetables in the saucepan and stir well to coat. Add the stock, tomatoes, chickpeas and sugar. Bring to the boil, cover and simmer gently for 30 minutes, or until the vegetables are tender.

2 Divide the soup in two, leaving half in the saucepan and buzzing the other half in a food processor or with a hand-held liquidiser to make a coarse-textured purée. Stir the purée back into the saucepan. This gives the soup a lovely texture. Add the coriander and lemon juice and heat through. Put a dollop of crème fraîche on top of each serving.

Five-a-Day Soup (Vegetable and Bacon Soup)

Serves 5–6

This wonderful soup follows the healthy advice of including five different vegetables in your diet every day. If preferred, liquidise or mash the cooked vegetables to make a thick purée soup. The rashers can also be omitted if preferred. Serve with Greek-style yoghurt and crusty bread.

You will need:

4–6 rashers, back or streaky

2–3 tablespoons olive oil

I large onion, chopped

2 cloves of garlic, crushed or chopped

I large carrot, diced

2 large potatoes, diced

2 sticks celery, chopped

salt and freshly ground black pepper

$1/2$ level teaspoon herbes de Provence or mixed herbs

I bay leaf (optional)

$1/4$ teaspoon hot chilli powder or cayenne pepper (optional)

900ml (I $1/2$ pints) chicken or vegetable stock (use only I stock cube; see note)

I x 400 g (14 oz) tin chopped tomatoes

To serve:

2–3 tablespoons chopped fresh parsley

Greek-style yoghurt or fromage frais

NOTE: I CHICKEN STOCK CUBE IS ENOUGH WHEN THE RASHERS ARE INCLUDED. IF RASHERS ARE OMITTED, 2 STOCK CUBES WILL BE REQUIRED FOR A GOOD FLAVOUR.

---

1 Chop the rashers and fry in $1/2$ tablespoon of the olive oil in a large saucepan until lightly golden.
2 Add the remaining oil and the onion and garlic to the rashers and fry gently for a few minutes, until soft. Add in the rest of the vegetables, seasoning with salt and pepper and adding the herbs and spices. Stir them through the oil and onions for about 3 minutes over a medium heat. Add the stock and tomatoes and bring to the boil. Cover with a lid and simmer gently, stirring occasionally, for 30 minutes, until the vegetables are tender. Check the seasoning and remove the bay leaf.

3 Stir the parsley through the soup and serve. Spoonfuls of Greek yoghurt can be served on top of each bowl of soup.

NOTE: IF WISHED, LIQUIDISE THE VEGETABLES TO MAKE A PURÉE OF THE SOUP. REHEAT BEFORE SERVING.

Variation:

For a totally different finish, omit the tin of tomatoes from the above recipe. When the vegetables are tender, blend 300 ml ($^1/_2$ pint) milk into 4 rounded teaspoons of cornflour and add to the cooked soup. Bring to the boil, stirring all the time. This thickens the soup a little, leaving the chopped vegetables intact. Serve sprinkled with the chopped parsley.

Potato and Anchovy Soup

Serves 5–6

On their own, potatoes are somewhat bland, so the strong flavour of the anchovies gives a subtle, salty flavour to the soup. If preferred, use chorizo, the spicy Spanish sausage. No other spices are used. If liked, a little spinach (frozen or fresh) can be added towards the end of the cooking time, which gives the soup extra nutrition and good colour.

You will need:

1 tablespoon olive oil

1 onion, finely chopped

1 clove of garlic, chopped

1 x 50 g (2 oz) tin anchovy fillets, drained OR 175–225 g (6–8 oz) chorizo, sliced

700 g (1½ lb) potatoes, peeled and diced

1.1 litres (2 pints) stock

1 fresh bay leaf

2–3 sprigs of fresh thyme or ½ teaspoon dried thyme

salt and freshly ground black pepper

110 g (4 oz) frozen chopped spinach (optional; see note)

To serve:

Greek-style yoghurt, fromage frais or crème fraîche

crusty bread

NOTE: A CUBE OF FROZEN SPINACH (THAWED) CAN BE ADDED TO THE SOUP. IF USING FRESH SPINACH, WASH, SHRED FINELY AND ADD DIRECTLY INTO THE SOUP AND BRING TO THE BOIL. THE SPINACH WILL LOSE MOST OF ITS VOLUME WHEN COOKED.

---

1 Put the olive oil into a heavy-based saucepan. Gently fry the onion and garlic for a few minutes to soften without browning. If using the sliced chorizo, add it to the onion at this stage and cook gently with the lid on for 1–2 minutes to release the flavour and the oils. Do not allow to brown.

2 Add in the potatoes, then add the stock, herbs and salt and pepper. Bring to the boil, cover with a lid and simmer gently for about 30 minutes, until the potatoes are tender. If using the anchovies, chop them finely and add to the soup at this stage.

3 Bring to the boil, stirring, and the anchovies will seem to disappear. Remove the bay leaf and thyme stalks. If using spinach, add it now and bring just to the boil to heat through.

4 A spoonful of yoghurt can be placed on top of each serving if liked. Serve with some crusty bread.

NOTE: I USE ROOSTER POTATOES FOR THIS SOUP BECAUSE THEY'RE FLOURY YET DON'T TURN TO MUSH WHEN COOKED.

Spicy Carrot Soup

Serves 4–5

This combination of ingredients gives a new twist to carrot soup. Inspired by a recipe of Paul Gayler, which he describes as an Asian soup, the ingredients include finely diced carrots flavoured with lemongrass, ginger and coconut milk. The final touch is to serve a little nest of crispy fried noodles on top of each serving. I took Tony Gavin's advice and fried the noodles for the topping in a little sesame oil rather than bland sunflower oil.

You will need:

25 g (1 oz) butter

2 cloves of garlic, crushed

1 heaped teaspoon Thai curry paste (red or yellow)

400 g (14 oz) carrots, peeled and diced neatly and finely

1 onion, finely chopped

2 sticks of lemongrass, outer layer discarded and grated finely

2.5 cm (1 inch) piece of fresh ginger, peeled and grated (about 1–2 teaspoons)

salt and freshly ground black pepper

1 level teaspoon ground coriander

700 ml (1¼ pint) vegetable stock

juice of ½ lime

200 ml (7 fl oz) coconut milk

To serve:

50–75 g (2–3 oz) egg noodles, cooked according to packet directions and well drained

a little sesame oil or sunflower oil

2 spring onions, finely chopped

4 lime wedges (optional)

1 Heat the butter in a heavy-based saucepan. Add the garlic and curry paste and cook together for 30 seconds. Add the carrots, onion, lemongrass and ginger and season with salt and pepper and the coriander. Cook gently, stirring together for 1–2 minutes. Pour in the stock, add the lime juice and bring to the boil. Reduce the heat and simmer for 10–15 minutes, until the carrots are bite tender. Add the coconut milk and cook for another 1–2 minutes.

2 Fry the cooked noodles in small batches, using sesame or sunflower oil or a combination of both. When crispy, lift out with a slotted spoon onto paper kitchen towels.

3 Serve the soup in individual bowls and at the last minute put a small nest of crispy noodles on top and scatter the spring onions over. Serve a wedge of lime with each bowl for guests to squeeze into their soup.

French Onion Soup

Serves 5–6

A real classic, French onion soup is a clever one. Just take a few onions and some stock, top with bread and cheese and you have a mouth-watering, warming and inexpensive soup. Add a little wine and a dash of brandy, and you have the real thing! This isn't a speedy soup, as long, slow cooking brings out the flavour of the onions.

Serve the soup in ovenproof bowls and put in the oven to let the cheese melt. A quick blast under the grill is then enough to brown the top.

You will need:

50 g (2 oz) butter

1 tablespoon olive oil

700–900g (1½–2lb) onions, sliced thinly (not chopped)

2 teaspoons sugar

salt and freshly ground black pepper

2 cloves of garlic, chopped

1.1–1.4 litres (2–2½ pints) hot beef stock (see note)

150 ml (¼ pint) dry white wine, cider or vermouth

2 tablespoons grated raw onion (optional)

4 tablespoons brandy (optional)

a little French mustard (optional)

To serve:

1–2 slices French bread per person, cut 2.5 cm (1 inch) thick (toasted if you like)

150 g (5 oz) grated cheese, preferably Gruyère

1 tablespoon melted butter

NOTE: YOU CAN USE A COMBINATION OF BEEF AND CHICKEN STOCK CUBES TO MAKE A GOOD STOCK QUICKLY.

1 Heat the butter and oil together in a heavy-based saucepan. Add the onions and stir until they are glistening with the butter. Partially cover with a lid at a tilt and cook gently for about 10 minutes, until the onions have softened. Remove the lid and sprinkle in the sugar, adding the garlic and salt and pepper to taste. Stir well. Continue to cook, uncovered, for another 40 minutes, stirring frequently to prevent burning. By now, the onions should be a deep golden-brown colour.

2 Add the hot stock and and the wine (or cider or vermouth). Simmer with the lid on for 20–30 minutes, then check the seasoning.

3 To serve, first heat the oven to 210°C/425°F/gas 7. Stir the grated onion, brandy and French mustard into the soup (if you're using them). Ladle the soup into ovenproof bowls and stand them on a baking tray. Place one or two slices of French bread on top of each bowl. Scatter the grated cheese generously over the top. Drizzle the melted butter over and bake for 10–20 minutes, until the cheese melts. Finish under a hot grill for 1–2 minutes to brown the top if you like. (Cheese cools slowly!) For speed, simply grill the cheese on the bread and put on top of the bowls of soup.

Roasted Mushroom Soup

Serves 4-6

Roasting the mushrooms in the oven before making the soup intensifies the flavour.

You will need:

500g (1 lb 2 oz) mushrooms, sliced

1 medium onion chopped

2 cloves of garlic, chopped

1 medium floury potato, peeled and chopped

1 stick tender celery, chopped finely

2–4 tablespoons olive oil

$^1/_2$ tablespoon soy sauce or Worcestershire sauce

juice of $^1/_2$ lemon (approximately)

salt and freshly ground black pepper

700 ml (1$^1/_4$ pints) chicken stock

$^1/_4$–$^1/_2$ teaspoon herbes de Provence

pinch of nutmeg

300 ml ($^1/_2$ pint) milk

3 level teaspoons cornflour (or use kneaded butter; see note)

150 ml (5 fl oz) cream (hold back a little for the soup bowls)

NOTE: TO MAKE KNEADED BUTTER, MASH 25 G (1 OZ) EACH OF BUTTER AND FLOUR INTO A PASTE. DROP LITTLE PIECES INTO THE BRISKLY SIMMERING COOKED SOUP WHILE STIRRING BRISKLY UNTIL THE REQUIRED THICKNESS HAS BEEN ACHIEVED.

---

1 Preheat the oven to 200°C/400°F/gas 6.

2 Spread the sliced mushrooms over a wide baking or roasting tin. Use two tins if necessary, as the layer of vegetables should not be too deep. Scatter the onion, garlic, potato and celery over them. Sprinkle the vegetables generously with the olive oil, some soy or Worcestershire sauce and the lemon juice and season with salt and pepper.

3 Cover the tray with foil and roast in the oven for 10 minutes, then lift off the foil and roast for another 10–15 minutes.

4 Empty the contents of the baking tin into a saucepan. Add the stock, herbes de Provence and nutmeg. Bring to the boil, then simmer gently until the potato is tender.

5 Strain off the mushrooms and vegetables, returning the liquid to the saucepan. Buzz the vegetable mixture in a food processor or liquidiser to chop very finely, then return to the soup in the saucepan.

6 Blend the milk into the cornflour, then add to the soup. Bring to the boil again to thicken sufficiently. Add the cream and simmer gently for a few minutes. Check the seasoning, adding extra lemon juice if liked.

7 Serve in soup bowls with a little of the remaining cream poured on the top.

CHAPTER 4

Salads and Vegetables

Vegetables continue to grow in importance in our diets – five a day is the battle cry of nutrition experts. It's good advice when you consider that variety is so important in a healthy diet. You don't have to be a vegetarian to enjoy vegetable dishes. There was a time not so long ago when onions, cabbage, carrots and potatoes were the standard vegetable fare in Ireland, but now we have all manner of vegetables to choose from.

Tomatoes and peppers, the vegetables that seem to bring the sunshine of the Mediterranean into our kitchens, aren't true natives of the area but are imports resulting from Columbus's travels. The Spaniards and Italians readily adopted these vegetables into their cooking. The French were more reluctant, initially using the new tomato, or pomme d'amour, as an ornamental plant. It wasn't until the 20th century that tomatoes became popular in England and Ireland, and the inclusion of peppers in our cooking is really quite recent indeed.

Mediterranean Vegetable Stacks

Serves 4

Goat's cheese would be the first choice for this recipe, as it combines so well with these vegetables, but other cheese can be used if preferred (e.g. feta, mozzarella or a combination of both). Grilled or fried, the sliced vegetables are layered on toasted bread with the cheese on top, then baked in the oven. This recipe can be used as a starter or main dish depending on the size of the serving.

You will need:

For the stacks:

4 slices of bread, cut into circles (small for a starter, larger for a main dish)

3–6 tablespoons olive oil

1 fat clove of garlic

4 slices of courgette, cut lengthways

4 slices of aubergine

4 slices of a large tomato

4 pieces of roasted red pepper (see note)

salt and freshly ground black pepper

4 round slices of goat's cheese (if very small, use 2 slices per serving)

For the French dressing:

3 tablespoons extra virgin olive oil

1 tablespoon balsamic vinegar

salt and freshly ground black pepper

$\frac{1}{2}$ teaspoon French mustard

$\frac{1}{2}$ teaspoon sugar

To serve:

4 handfuls of dressed mixed salad leaves

25 g (1 oz) toasted walnuts

NOTE: USE 1 LARGE RED PEPPER (OR 2 SMALL ONES) AND GRILL OR ROAST UNTIL THE SKIN BLACKENS. COVER WITH A BOWL OR FOIL TO KEEP THE HEAT IN, WHICH LOOSENS THE SKIN. WHEN COOL ENOUGH TO HANDLE, SCRAPE OFF THE SKIN, AVOIDING THE TEMPTATION TO WASH THE PEPPER, AS THIS ALSO WASHES OFF THE NATURAL TASTY JUICES. CUT THE PEPPER INTO FOUR SECTIONS, DISCARDING THE STALK AND SEEDS.

1 Heat the oven to 200°C/400°F/gas 6.

2 Place the circles of bread on a baking tin. Drizzle with a little of the olive oil and rub with the clove of garlic (keep the garlic clove to use in a moment). Bake for 3–5 minutes, until lightly toasted.

3 Heat the remaining oil in a pan. Add the clove of garlic, fry gently for 1–2 minutes to flavour the oil, then lift it out and discard or use elsewhere.

4 Fry the courgette slices in the flavoured oil until golden. Lift out and fry the aubergines, adding more oil if needed. Season all the vegetable slices lightly with salt and pepper.

5 Make four stacks of alternating sliced vegetables on top of each round of baked toast, starting with the aubergine and finishing with the goat's cheese on top. These stacks can be prepared in advance and kept covered in the kitchen (not cold in the fridge). Just before serving, bake in the oven for 15 minutes, until the cheese browns on top and the vegetables are warmed through.

6 To make the dressing, simply put all the ingredients in a screwtop jar and shake well to mix. Toss lightly with the salad.

7 Serve each stack on a plate with the dressed salad alongside and the walnuts scattered on top of everything.

Mediterranean Vegetable Mixture

Serves 5–6

This tasty vegetable mixture can be served on its own or used in the vegetable lasagne recipe on p.197.

You will need:

1 large onion, sliced thinly

2–3 tablespoons olive oil

2–4 cloves of garlic, chopped

225 g (8 oz) mushrooms, sliced

1 medium courgette (about 275 g/10 oz), chopped

1 large red pepper (about 225 g/8 oz), deseeded and chopped (see note)

1 x 400 g (14 oz) tin chopped tomatoes

salt and freshly ground black pepper

1 level teaspoon oregano

2 teaspoons sugar

2–3 teaspoons tomato purée

2–3 teaspoons tomato relish

To serve:

natural yoghurt and crusty bread

NOTE: IDEALLY, SKIN THE PEPPER BEFORE USING IT (SEE P.64).

---

1 Heat the oil in a big pan or saucepan. Fry the onion for 1 minute, then add all the remaining ingredients.
2 Bring to the boil, cover with the lid and cook for 20 minutes, until tender. Serve with natural yoghurt and crusty bread or use as a filling for vegetable lasagne (see p.197) or for crêpes.

Greek-style Salad

Serves 3–4

Marinate the feta cheese in the dressing first to make this version of the classic Greek salad. Use crusty bread to soak up the tasty juices.

You will need:

150 g (5 oz) feta cheese

3 tomatoes (about 275 g/10 oz), cut into wedges and then halved

1 small green pepper (raw or roasted), chopped

$\frac{1}{2}$ crisp cucumber, cut into bite-sized chunks

10–12 black olives, pitted

1 small onion, thinly sliced

salt and freshly ground black pepper

$\frac{1}{4}$–$\frac{1}{2}$ teaspoon coriander

$\frac{1}{4}$ teaspoon thyme or oregano

pinch sugar

For the dressing/marinade:

60 ml (4 tablespoons) olive oil

1 tablespoon lemon juice

Salt and freshly ground black pepper

$\frac{1}{4}$ teaspoon oregano

$\frac{1}{4}$ teaspoon cumin

To serve:

crusty bread

1 Mix together the dressing ingredients in a bowl large enough to eventually hold all the salad ingredients (do not use a metal bowl). Cut the feta cheese into small cubes and add to the marinade. Cover and set aside.

2 Put the tomatoes into the bowl with the feta cheese. Add the green pepper, cucumber, olives and onion. Season with salt and pepper and mix in the coriander and thyme or oregano. Toss everything gently together and serve in the bowl, accompanied with crusty bread.

Baked Butternut Squash

Serves 2–4

This recipe can be served as a main dish or as a vegetable accompaniment. If I find it too hard to cut the squash into two with a big knife, I simply use a small sharp knife to cut the skin all the way around; it's then easier to cut in half.

You will need:

1 butternut squash, about 700 g (1½ lb)

olive oil

salt and freshly ground black pepper

½ teaspoon paprika

3 tablespoons chopped fresh chives

3 tablespoons crème fraîche

50g (2 oz) cashew nuts or pine nuts, toasted or fried until golden in a little olive oil

1–2 thick slices of white bread, crust removed and crumbled into breadcrumbs

generous pinch of dried oregano

generous knob of butter, melted

25g (1 oz) Parmesan, freshly grated

1 Preheat the oven to 200°C/400°F/gas 6.
2 Halve the squash lengthways, then scoop out the seeds and surrounding fibres. Brush the cut surface with olive oil and season with salt and pepper. Put in a roasting tin, using a little crumpled foil underneath to steady the halves if needed. Pour a shallow layer of water into the tin to make a steamy atmosphere in the oven.
3 Cover the squash loosely with a piece of foil and bake for 40–50 minutes, until the squash is tender when pierced with a fork, but not collapsing.
4 Drain off the water. Transfer the squash to a board and leave until cool enough to handle, then carefully scrape out the flesh into a bowl, leaving a thin border of flesh on the skin. Don't pierce the skin!
5 Mix the paprika, chives, crème fraîche and nuts into the squash flesh and season. Carefully pile the mixture back into the squash shells.
6 Season the breadcrumbs with salt, pepper and oregano and mix with the butter and some of the Parmesan. Sprinkle generously over the squash shells, scattering more Parmesan over the top. Bake for 15 minutes, until lightly browned.

Variation:

Coarsely chop 75–110 g (3–4 oz) feta cheese and mix it with the butternut squash and the crème fraiche and nuts. Continue as above and bake as directed.

Butternut Squash Purée

Serves 3–4

This vibrant orange purée makes a wonderful vegetable accompaniment to many meat dishes. All squashes respond well to spices. Other suitable spices you might like to try are allspice, cinnamon, ginger and cardamom. Great to serve with autumn casseroles and with Christmas meals.

You will need:
1 butternut squash, about 700 g (1 1/2 lb)
olive oil
salt and freshly ground black pepper
generous knob of butter, melted
1/2 teaspoon finely grated root ginger
1/2 teaspoon coriander
2–3 tablespoons cream or crème fraîche

1 Roast the butternut squash as described on p.68. When tender, scoop out the flesh completely and put into a saucepan with a knob of melted butter. Add the grated ginger, ground coriander, some salt and pepper, the cream or crème fraîche and mash to a smooth purée.

THERE ARE 15 COUNTRIES surrounding the Mediterranean coast, and while we are familiar with the dishes of France, Italy and Spain, the countries of the Middle East, such as Turkey, Syria and Lebanon, are a treasure trove of recipes. A few of the local dishes are already known worldwide, such as kebabs and tabbouleh, but there are many others just waiting to be tried.

Imam Bayildi ('The Imam Fainted')

Serves 4 as a starter or vegetable accompaniment or 2 as a main course

The imam in question apparently passed out from pure pleasure when he tasted this much-loved Turkish dish. The halved aubergines are scooped out and filled again with a tasty mixture of lightly spiced vegetables, then baked. If serving as a main dish, allow two halves per person, accompanied with a salad and bread and some natural yoghurt to spoon over. This is also suitable as a starter or as a vegetable accompaniment.

You will need:
2 large aubergines (see note)
3–6 tablespoons olive oil
1 onion, finely chopped
1 fat clove of garlic, chopped
1 large red pepper, deseeded and chopped
1 x 400 g (14 oz) tin chopped tomatoes
45 g (1 1/2 oz) raisins
1 level teaspoon brown sugar
1/2 level teaspoon ground cinnamon
salt and freshly ground black pepper
1–2 tablespoon pine nuts, toasted or lightly fried until golden in a spoon of olive oil
1 tablespoon chopped fresh parsley or coriander

To serve:
1 tablespoon toasted pine kernels
chopped fresh parsley

NOTE: MANY RECIPES RECOMMEND SALTING THE AUBERGINES TO DRAW OUT SOME OF THEIR BITTER JUICES (THE FRENCH CALL THIS PROCESS DÉGORGER). THIS IS NOT ALWAYS NECESSARY, ESPECIALLY IF THE AUBERGINES ARE RIPE. THIS CAN BE JUDGED BY LOOKING UNDER THE CALYX (THE GREEN 'STAR' WHERE THE FRUIT JOINS THE STEM). IF THE SKIN IS PURE WHITE, THE FRUIT IS RIPE. IF GREEN, IT CAN BE LEFT

FOR A FEW DAYS AND IT WILL RIPEN, EVEN OFF THE PLANT. OVER-RIPE FRUIT IS EASY TO SPOT TOO — IT WILL BE LIGHTER AND SPONGIER AND WHEN YOU CUT IT OPEN THE FLESH WILL BE FULL OF SEEDS. IF UNDER-RIPE OR OVER-RIPE, THE AUBERGINES MAY BE SOMEWHAT BITTER. TO DRAW OFF THE BITTERNESS, SCATTER SALT LIBERALLY ON THE CHOPPED, SCOOPED-OUT FLESH AND INSIDE THE HOLLOWED SKINS. LEAVE FOR 30 MINUTES TO DRAIN, THEN RINSE OFF THE SALT AND PAT DRY WITH PAPER KITCHEN TOWELS.

1   Preheat the oven to 190°C/375°F/gas 5.
2   Cut the aubergines in half lengthways, right through the stalk. Cut down into the flesh about 1 cm ($^1/_2$ inch) in from the edge all around, and cut the rest of the flesh in a criss-cross fashion, as this helps when scooping out the flesh. Take care not to go through to the skin – there should be about 1 cm ($^1/_2$ inch) of flesh left on the skin.
3   Chop the scooped-out flesh and leave to one side while you prepare the filling. (If you wish, sprinkle both the flesh and the halves with salt; see note, above.)
4   Heat 2 tablespoons of the oil in a pan over a moderate heat. Fry the aubergine halves gently on both sides for a few minutes, then transfer to an ovenproof dish. Add more oil to the pan and sauté the onion and garlic for a few minutes, until soft and slightly golden. Add the chopped aubergine flesh and cook for a further few minutes, stirring. Add the remaining ingredients and fry gently, stirring, for about 5 minutes. Taste and season if required.
5   Fill the aubergine halves with the mixture. Pour a little boiling water into the dish (approximately 1 cm/$^1/_2$ inch deep). Cover the dish loosely with foil and bake in the oven for 30–45 minutes, until the aubergine flesh is soft when tested with a skewer. Remove the foil for the last 10–15 minutes of baking. Serve hot, scattered with the pine nuts and the chopped parsley.

Variation:

For an Italian twist, omit the red pepper and the cinnamon. Instead, use 150 g (5 oz) frozen chopped spinach (thawed), a few pinches of nutmeg and 75 g (3 oz) coarsely crumbled feta cheese. Add these to the fried onion mixture and proceed as above. Sprinkle the tops with some grated mozzarella cheese and bake as outlined above.

Baked Potatoes

Serves 4

A floury potato, such as Rooster, Maris Piper or Kerr's Pink, is the best choice for baked potatoes. Potatoes bake much better when they are not wrapped in foil. Oven baking results in a nice crispy skin, though microwave cooking is much faster.

You will need:
4 large floury potatoes (approx. 350–450g/12–16 oz each)
a little olive oil
salt and freshly ground black pepper

1 Wash and dry the potatoes and prick the skin in several places to prevent them from bursting as they cook. Brush with oil and season with salt and pepper. Put on a baking tin.

2 **To bake in the oven:** Preheat the oven to 210°C/425°F/gas 7. Bake for 1–1¼ hours or until tender. Keep an eye on them, because potatoes get too dried out if overcooked. Test by piercing a skewer into the centre, which should be tender. The skins will get lovely and crispy on the outside. Serve as required.

3 **To cook in the microwave:** Put the prepared potatoes into the microwave and cook on the high setting for 5–10 minutes. Microwaves vary, so check frequently to prevent overcooking. If overcooked, the potatoes become dried out and leathery. Practice will tell you how long it will take. The size of the potatoes determines how quickly they will cook. Don't put too many in the microwave at one time – unlike the oven, the more you put in, the longer it takes to cook. Serve as required.

Soufflé Baked Potatoes

Serves 4

When baked, the potatoes are halved, the flesh scooped out and the skins returned to the oven to crisp. Meanwhile, the flesh is coarsely mashed together with a number of ingredients as well as stiffly beaten egg whites. This mixture is then spooned back into the skins and baked until delightfully golden on top. This makes a hearty snack or a light meal.

You will need:
4 large floury potatoes, baked as outlined above
salt and freshly ground black pepper

2 eggs, separated

3–4 tablespoons cream

1 teaspoon wholegrain mustard

75 g (3 oz) cherry tomatoes, halved

2–3 spring onions, chopped

40 g (1½ oz) grated white mature cheddar cheese

1 tablespoon chopped chives

1 tablespoon chopped parsley

a little extra grated cheese for the top (optional)

1. After baking the potatoes as described on p.74, remove from the oven and reduce the temperature to 200°C/400°F/gas 6.
2. Cut each potato in half and scoop the flesh into a bowl. Return the skins (half potato shells) to the oven for 5 minutes or so, to crisp lightly. Mash the potato flesh coarsely using a fork. Season with salt and pepper.
3. In a separate small bowl, mix together the egg yolks, cream and mustard, then add to the mashed potato and mix well. Add the remaining ingredients and mix gently but thoroughly.
4. In a separate clean, dry bowl, whisk the egg whites until stiff. Add to the potato mixture and mix in gently but thoroughly.
5. Spoon the mashed potato mixture into the crispy half potato skins, piling it in generously. Scatter a little grated cheese on top. Return the tin to the oven for 15–20 minutes, until the tops are golden brown. Serve immediately, accompanied with a little mayonnaise if desired.

MAKING YOUR OWN MAYONNAISE is somewhat like making your own pasta – a joy when you have time. Experimenting with various oils and vinegars will produce a range of flavours.

It helps to understand the secrets of this procedure. Needless to say, since the egg yolks are used raw, it's important to use best-quality, fresh, free-range eggs. It's also important to bring all the ingredients to room temperature before you start.

Beating the oil into the egg yolks is necessary to reduce the oil into tiny droplets so that it will blend in. At the start, the oil must literally be added a drop at a time and whisked thoroughly into the egg yolks after each drop. After some time, the tiny droplets that have been formed will actually encourage the mixing in of the remaining oil so that it can be added in slightly more generous amounts. However, don't get too confident and start lashing in the oil, since the yolks can only absorb it a little at a time.

Olive oil used alone doesn't make good mayonnaise, particularly extra virgin olive oil. I well remember my futile attempts to beat the extra virgin olive oil into the egg yolks, which would just end up as a yellow puddle in the bowl. You need to use groundnut (peanut) oil or sunflower oil first, as it's lighter and will break down into the tiny droplets required much more easily, after which olive oil can be added. With practice, you can experiment with using flavoured oils, trying a hint of walnut or hazelnut oil for flavour.

When made, cover the mayonnaise with clingfilm pressed right down onto the surface to prevent the air from discolouring it and store in the fridge for up to three or four days.

Basic Homemade Mayonnaise

Makes approx 300 ml (10 fl oz)

A balloon whisk is the traditional tool to use, but I find a hand-held electric beater saves a lot of the effort required to do the beating!

You will need:
100 ml (3¹/₂ fl oz) groundnut or sunflower oil
3 medium egg yolks or 2 large ones
small pinch of salt
¹/₄ teaspoon Dijon mustard
1 dessertspoon white wine vinegar
200 ml (7 fl oz) olive oil (not extra virgin)
freshly ground white or black pepper
fresh lemon juice to taste (optional)

1 Put the groundnut oil into a jug. Put the egg yolks into a medium bowl and add the salt, mustard and vinegar and whisk together until well blended.

2 Start adding the groundnut oil, drop by drop, whisking constantly. By the time approximately half of the oil has been added, the mixture should be getting somewhat creamy and slightly thickened. This means that the emulsion is beginning to form and you can add the oil ever so slightly faster. When all the groundnut oil has been added, transfer the olive oil into the jug and continue adding to the mix, possibly a teaspoon at a time. If the mayonnaise seems to be getting too thick, whisk in a little lemon juice or a spoon or two of hot water.

3 When all the oil has been added, check the seasoning, adding vinegar or lemon juice and salt and pepper as required.

4 If you want to soften the consistency of the mayonnaise, simply whisk in dribbles of warm water until you get the texture you want.

NOTE: IF THE MAYONNAISE CURDLES WHILE YOU'RE MAKING IT — THAT IS, IT SUDDENLY BECOMES QUITE THIN OR THE OIL STARTS TO SEPARATE OUT IF YOU'VE LEFT IT FOR SOME TIME — SIMPLY GET ANOTHER BOWL, PUT ANOTHER EGG YOLK INTO IT AND START WHISKING IT INTO THE CURDLED MAYONNAISE, A HALF A TEASPOON AT A TIME, TO START THE EMULSIFYING PROCESS AGAIN.

Variations

The following flavourings can be added either to the above homemade mayonnaise or to 300 ml (10 fl oz) of shop-bought mayonnaise.

Garlic mayonnaise

Add in 1–3 crushed cloves of garlic (depending on how much you like it!). The garlic can be added to the egg yolks at the start of the process, or they can be whisked into the made mayonnaise at the end. This is good served as a dip with cruditiés of raw vegetables or with fish.

Herb mayonnaise

Use either one or a combination of soft-leaved herbs such as parsley, basil, mint or tarragon. Experiment with flavours. Try 2–3 tablespoons of chopped fresh dill (only) in the mayonnaise. If liked, add a squeeze of fresh lime juice and serve with fish.

Anchovy mayonnaise

Anchovies give a salty kick to the mayonnaise. Finely chop about 4 fillets of tinned anchovies and whisk into the made mayonnaise.

Tuna mayonnaise

Drain a 140 g (5 oz) tin of tuna and add to the mayonnaise with a little fresh lemon juice and 1 tablespoon of drained capers and whisk together. Season with freshly ground black pepper. This makes a wonderful spread on egg or chicken sandwiches.

Crunchy Cajun Cauliflower

Serves 4–5

When overcooked, cauliflower creates a rather unpleasant smell in the kitchen, so watch it carefully. The crunch of the spicy breadcrumbs contrasts nicely with the cauliflower.

You will need:

1 medium cauliflower

1.1 litres (about 2 pints) water

$^1/_2$–1 stock cube, chicken or vegetable (optional)

50 g (2 oz) butter

1 tablespoon olive oil

4–5 tablespoons breadcrumbs

1 clove of garlic, thinly sliced

salt and freshly ground black pepper

1–2 teaspoons Cajun seasoning

1 Separate the cauliflower into individual florets, cutting some in half if necessary to make them even-sized. Wash in cold water and drain.
2 Bring the water to a boil in a wide saucepan. (Ideally, use a wide saucepan so that the cauliflower florets can fit in one layer, barely covered with the stock.) Dissolve the stock cube in the boiling water, then add the cauliflower florets. Bring back to the boil and then simmer briskly, with the lid on at a tilt, for 5–10 minutes or until almost tender, not forgetting that it will get another blast of heat in the frying pan. Drain well (you could save the stock that remains and use it for a soup if you like).
3 Melt half the butter and 1 teaspoon of the oil in a frying pan over a moderate to high heat. When it's foaming, add the breadcrumbs and fry until crisp. Transfer to a small bowl and wipe the pan.
4 Heat the remaining butter and oil together over a moderate heat. Add the garlic and the cauliflower florets. Season with salt and pepper, sprinkle with the Cajun seasoning and fry for 3–4 minutes, tossing gently, until the cauliflower is flecked with gold.
5 Transfer to a warmed serving dish. Scatter the breadcrumbs over and toss through, adding extra salt and pepper if required.

Variation:

Instead of the Cajun seasoning, try $^1/_2$ –1 tablespoon finely chopped fresh thyme leaves and $^1/_2$ teaspoon finely grated lemon zest.

INDIA IS ONE OF the largest and most populous countries in the world and thus has a great diversity of cuisines. It's larger than the whole of Europe. Like Europe, the northern areas are colder and wetter, which favours rearing cattle and growing wheat, and this is reflected in the region's dishes. The south, on the other hand, is notable for its use of vegetables, fruit and fish (around the coast), much like the Mediterranean. Indian cooking is interesting for its rules and regulations. As well as regional variations, the country has at least four major faiths – Hinduism, Buddhism, Islam and Christianity – each with its own dietary laws. There are also many fast days, days on which only certain foods are eaten.

The generous use of many spices is the common denominator between the various religious and regional cuisines.

Generally speaking, an Indian meal consists of a meat, fish or vegetable dish, bread and/or rice and a pulse dish (e.g. lentils) as well as a yoghurt relish and fresh chutney. Fruit rather than dessert may be served at the end of the meal. Sweets are sometimes served on festive occasions.

Everyone in India, from princes to villagers, eats curries. The origin of the word 'curry' is the Tamil word 'kari', which originally meant a thin spicy sauce. The British colonials adopted the word 'curry' and applied one name to all manner of curry dishes.

Most of the spices used in Indian cooking were originally chosen as much for their medicinal and antiseptic properties as for their flavour, which were important considerations in the days before refrigeration. Traditionally, the spices were freshly ground each day, but this was very time consuming and is now more often done once a week or the spices are bought in a store. Experiment with different curry powders to find the one you like, or mix your own favourite spices. Rooting around in the back of the kitchen cupboard for that old jar of curry powder isn't going to produce an aromatic curry. Pay attention to the use-by dates on all packets of spices and curry powders and buy your spices in a shop that has a good turnover.

Potato and Cumin Curry (Aloo Jeera)

Serves 4–6

This dish is from the south of India, which has many wonderful potato recipes. The colours, texture and flavour of this dish are delicious. It can be served on its own as a light lunch dish, accompanied with a yoghurt and cucumber relish, or with other vegetable, meat or fish dishes. Very floury potatoes aren't suitable for this recipe, as they would just become mushy; use moderately waxy potatoes instead. Rooster potatoes are a good choice, as they soften easily and yet hold their shape relatively well.

You will need:

500 g (1 lb 2 oz) potatoes, peeled and diced

2–4 tablespoons vegetable oil

4 cloves of garlic, crushed

thumb-sized piece of fresh ginger, peeled and grated

2–3 large shallots or 1 onion, finely chopped

2–3 long, thin green or red chillies, deseeded and finely chopped

1 teaspoon ground turmeric

1 tablespoon black mustard seeds

$^1/_2$–1 tablespoon ground coriander

$^1/_2$–1 tablespoon ground cumin

2 green cardamom pods, crushed – use seeds only

4 tomatoes, chopped

$^1/_2$–1 x 300 g (11 oz) tin chickpeas, drained

4 tablespoons water

salt and freshly ground black pepper

juice of 1 lemon

chopped fresh coriander

For the yoghurt and cucumber relish:

2 x 125 ml (4$^1/_2$ fl oz) cartons of natural yoghurt

salt and freshly ground black pepper

$^1/_2$ cup finely diced or grated cucumber

2–3 teaspoons mint, to taste

To serve:

naan bread and/or poppadoms

mango chutney

NOTE: It's a good idea to partly cook the diced potatoes in boiling salted water for 5–8 minutes to soften them. Drain well before adding to the pan with the spices.

1 Heat the oil in a heavy saucepan or large frying pan over a medium heat. Add the garlic and ginger and fry gently for a few seconds, until fragrant. Add the shallots and chillies, stirring together to soften the shallots. Stir in the turmeric, mustard seeds, ground coriander, cumin and cardamom seeds. Cook for about 1 minute, until the spices are fragrant.
2 Add the potatoes and stir through all the wonderful flavours. Finally, add the tomatoes, chickpeas and the 4 tablespoons of water. Season the mixture well with salt and pepper.
3 Cover with a lid and continue cooking over a moderate heat for 15–20 minutes, until the potatoes are tender, stirring occasionally. Add a little extra water if necessary.
4 In the meantime, make the yoghurt and cucumber relish by mixing the yoghurt in a bowl with the salt and pepper. Add the cucumber and mint to taste.
5 When ready to serve, add the lemon juice and some of the chopped fresh coriander. Check for seasoning – you want a nice hot, spicy, slightly sweet, lemony and salty taste. Serve garnished with more chopped coriander. Accompany with mango chutney, naan bread and/or poppadoms and a dish of the yoghurt and cucumber relish.

Pommes Boulangère

Serves 3–4

This dish is a glimpse into French village history. Traditionally, the housewife would make up her dish of potatoes and then bring it to the local baker (boulanger), who would cook it in his large hot oven.

This recipe doesn't contain milk, cream or cheese, just stock, onion and herbs. The potatoes are very thinly sliced and layered with sliced onions and garlic that have been fried gently in butter and herbs. Arrange in layers and bake until delightfully golden on top. The layers can be made as shallow and wide or as deep and narrow as you like.

You will need:
50g (2 oz) butter
$^1/_2$ tablespoon olive oil
I onion, thinly sliced
I–2 cloves of garlic, chopped

leaves from 2–3 small sprigs of thyme or ¼–½ teaspoon dried thyme

2 bay leaves

1 tablespoon chopped parsley

700 g (1½ lb potatoes)

salt and freshly ground black pepper

425–600 ml (¾–1 pint) hot chicken or vegetable stock

NOTE: WASH THE POTATOES BEFORE (RATHER THAN AFTER) SLICING THEM TO CONSERVE THEIR NATURAL STARCH.

---

1 Preheat the oven to 190°C/375°F/gas 5. For a shallow, wide effect, use a flan dish about 25.5 cm (10 inches) in diameter and butter the base.
2 Melt the butter in a frying pan with the olive oil. Add the onion and garlic and fry gently for a few minutes, until soft and slightly golden. Stir in the herbs.
3 Peel the potatoes and slice very thinly, about 3 mm (⅛ inch) thick, using a sharp knife or grater, or, better still, a food processor.
4 Spread half the sliced potatoes in an even layer over the base, seasoning them with salt and pepper. Next, spread half the onion, butter and herb mixture in a layer over the potatoes. Then spread the rest of the potato slices in a layer on top, again seasoning well with salt and pepper. Pour in the hot stock – it should barely reach the top of the potatoes. Dribble any remaining butter mixture over the top.
5 Bake for about 1 hour, until the potatoes are soft when pierced with a skewer and the top is browned. Cover with foil if the top gets brown too soon.

Variation:

To make **potatoes savoyarde**, make the recipe as above but include 75–110 g (3–4 oz) of grated Gruyère cheese through the layers, with a little more sprinkled on top.

HOT SALADS MIGHT seem like a contradiction in terms, since most of us associate salads with raw vegetables. *Salades tièdes*, as the French call them, have their origins in the nouvelle cuisine movement of the 1970s, when the old traditional methods of French haute cuisine, with its heavy classic sauces, were cast aside in favour of more emphasis on fresh produce.

Warm Spicy Lamb Salad

Serves 2–3

You will need:
300 g (about 11 oz) leg of lamb steaks
1 teaspoon cinnamon
1 teaspoon cumin
1 teaspoon paprika
salt and freshly ground black pepper
olive oil for frying

For the salad:

1 bag mixed baby salad leaves

4–5 spring onions, thinly sliced

6 cherry tomatoes, halved

1 orange, peeled and divided into segments

5 cm (2 inch) cucumber, diced or sliced

honey dressing (see p.89)

1 Cut the fat off the meat and cut into thick finger-sized pieces.

2 Mix the spices and seasoning together in a plastic bag. Add the lamb and shake to coat with the spices. Remove the meat, shake off the excess spices and fry a few pieces at a time in a little hot oil for 3–5 minutes, until browned all over and cooked to the required doneness.

3 Mix the salad leaves with the spring onions, cherry tomatoes, orange segments and cucumber and toss with some of the honey dressing.

4 Divide the salad between two or three dinner plates. Spoon the hot fried lamb on top and serve.

NOTE: FOR MEMBRANE-FREE ORANGE SEGMENTS, PEEL THE ORANGE WITH A SHARP KNIFE AND REMOVE ALL THE PITH AND MEMBRANE. NOW INSERT THE KNIFE BETWEEN ONE SEGMENT AND ITS MEMBRANE COATING AND PUSH OUT THE SEGMENT. REPEAT FOR EACH SEGMENT. WORK OVER A PLATE TO CATCH THE JUICES.

Variation:

To make a warm **Cajun chicken salad**, substitute 2 skinless chicken fillets for the lamb and 2–3 teaspoons Cajun seasoning for the spices above. Cut the chicken fillets into finger-sized pieces and coat lightly with the Cajun spices. Fry in a little hot oil for 4–6 minutes, until cooked through. Serve as above.

Honey Dressing

Makes approx. 100 ml (3½ fl oz)

You will need:
3 tablespoons extra virgin olive oil
2 tablespoons vegetable oil
1–2 tablespoons balsamic vinegar
1 tablespoons fresh lemon juice
1–2 cloves of garlic, crushed (optional)
salt and freshly ground black pepper
1 generous teaspoon honey
1 teaspoon sugar
pinch of herbes de Provence
2 tablespoon cream

1 Put all ingredients into a screwtop jar and shake vigorously to mix (or whisk well together). This keeps in the fridge for up to a fortnight.

THE ROMANS WERE enthusiastic eaters of salads. Much like our present-day salads, they used a collection of raw vegetables such as lettuce, cucumber and chicory and tossed them in a dressing of oil and vinegar or sometimes brine. The Latin 'herba salata', which means 'salted herbs', is the origin of the word 'salad'. The Romans introduced salad to Britain, but its use declined after their departure, to be revived enthusiastically in the Middle Ages. However, Mrs Beeton wasn't so enthusiastic in the first edition of her cookbook in 1861, where she said, 'Lettuce is not very nutritious and should be sent to the table in a good gravy.'

Salad Niçoise

Serves 4 as a main lunch dish

Bring the Mediterranean to your table with this classic salad, a must in any cook's repertoire. Eat it outside in your garden, with crusty bread and a glass of wine. This salad originally included only raw vegetables, but nowadays cooked beans and cooked potatoes are often included. Ideally, serve on a platter or in a wide bowl rather than a deep one.

You will need:
350–450 g (12–16 oz) new potatoes, scrubbed and cooked
salt and freshly ground black pepper
1 small head of butterhead lettuce (or 2–3 little gems)
110 g (4 oz) green beans, cooked
1/2 small cucumber, chopped
4–6 spring onions, chopped
6 small ripe tomatoes, quartered
2 x 200 g (7 oz) tins tuna steak, drained
3 hardboiled eggs, quartered
1 small tin anchovies (optional)
50–75g (2–3 oz) black olives, pitted
2 tablespoons chopped parsley

For the dressing:
8 tablespoons olive oil
3–4 tablespoons wine vinegar
1 teaspoon sugar or honey
1/2 teaspoon Dijon mustard
salt and freshly ground black pepper
pinch of dried oregano

1　To prepare the dressing, simply shake all these ingredients together in a screwtop jar. Set aside.

2　While the cooked potatoes are still warm, halve or quarter them, depending on size, and put into a mixing bowl. Season well with salt and pepper and add a little of the dressing. Toss together and leave to cool.

3　Shred the lettuce into small pieces, toss with some more of the dressing and arrange in a layer over the serving platter. Scatter the prepared potatoes over the lettuce. Toss the green beans and cucumber in a little more of the dressing and scatter them on top of the potatoes. The spring onions and tomatoes can be scattered next over the top. Place the chunks of tuna fish and the eggs here and there over the top as well as the anchovies and olives.

4　Drizzle any remaining dressing to taste over the top of everything, seasoning a little more with salt and pepper if necessary. Sprinkle the parsley liberally over everything.

CHAPTER 5

Casseroles

It only stands to reason that we Irish, who live in a country where the days are short, dark, dank and cold for a few months of the year, would cry out for comforting dishes. Hot steaming casseroles to soothe and give sustenance, with all manner of ingredients, are just the thing.

Casseroles get their name from the vessel they were cooked in (usually covered ovenproof dishes). Of course, a good heavy saucepan, in which the casserole can simmer slowly for hours on top of the cooker, will do the job too.

It's worth remembering that a casserole/stew is even better when reheated the next day, as it allows the flavours to mellow together. I like to call it the Casserole Two-Step: on day one, prepare the casserole and allow it to cook slowly while you relax. On day two, simply reheat, and you have an instant meal!

NOTE: WINE AND OTHER ALCOHOLS ARE USED IN MANY RECIPES, BUT THE ALCOHOL CONTENT IS ALL DRIVEN OFF DURING THE LONG COOKING.

NOTE: WHEN BROWNING THE PIECES OF MEAT AS PREPARATION FOR A CASSEROLE, DO IT IN SMALL BATCHES, OTHERWISE THE TEMPERATURE OF THE PAN DROPS AND THE MEAT 'STEWS' RATHER THAN BROWNS.

Tips to thicken any liquid: Kneaded butter

Equal quantities of butter and flour are mashed together into a raw paste; usually about 50 g (2 oz) of each are used. Little bits of this paste are then dropped into the briskly simmering (almost boiling) liquid while stirring with a whisk until the desired thickness is achieved.

The kneaded butter can be stored in the fridge for 3–4 weeks.

Moroccan Lamb Tagine

Serves 5–6

The Arabs invaded Morocco in the 7th century and settled there, bringing with them their Eastern spices and introducing them into the local cuisine. The delightful flavour of this recipe is achieved by combining spices, herbs and dried fruit with lamb. The word 'tagine' means 'stew' and is also the name of the earthenware dish with a distinctive pointed conical cover in which this and many other stews are traditionally cooked (though any casserole or heavy saucepan is suitable).

Most tagine recipes suggest shoulder of lamb, as it has a particularly good flavour, though leg of lamb can also be used. Don't forget the special finish of toasted almonds and fresh mint. Serve with cooked basmati rice or couscous or simply mashed potatoes.

You will need:

800–900 g (1 3/4–2 lb) bite-sized chunks of lean lamb cut from the shoulder

For the dry marinade:

1 teaspoon ground cinnamon

1 teaspoon ground cumin

1–2 teaspoons grated fresh ginger

1/2 teaspoon paprika

1 medium onion, chopped

2 cloves of garlic, chopped

1–2 tablespoons chopped fresh coriander

salt and freshly ground black pepper

For the sauce:

3–4 tablespoons olive oil

1 large onion, chopped

1 clove of garlic, chopped

300 ml (1/2 pint) vegetable stock

1 x 400 g (14 oz) tin chopped tomatoes

1 tablespoon tomato purée

1–2 thin strips of orange peel, no white pith

50 g (2 oz) ready-to-eat apricots

50 g (2 oz) ready-to-eat prunes (stoneless)

1/2–1 teaspoon chopped fresh red chilli

To serve:

75 g (3 oz) whole blanched almonds

1–2 tablespoons chopped fresh mint

cooked basmati rice (allow 50 g/2 oz uncooked rice per serving) or the couscous pilaf on p.101

1 Put the lamb pieces into a bowl. In a separate bowl, combine all the dry marinade ingredients and mix well. Stir the marinade into the lamb, coating well. Cover and leave for at least 30 minutes, preferably longer (up to 3 hours). If keeping overnight, put in the fridge.

2 To make the sauce, heat the olive oil in a frying pan and fry the onion and garlic for 1–2 minutes, until soft. Lift out and transfer to a saucepan or casserole.

3 Fry the lamb (including the dry marinade) in small batches until the meat is lightly browned, then transfer to the saucepan. Add all the remaining sauce ingredients to the saucepan and bring to the boil. Cover with a lid and simmer gently for about 1 hour, or until the lamb is tender, reducing the heat if necessary.

4   Before serving, discard the orange peel. Fry the almonds until golden in a little olive oil, drain and stir into the stew along with the fresh mint. Serve with cooked basmati rice or couscous pilaf (p.101).

NOTE: IF YOU PREFER, YOU CAN COOK THIS IN THE OVEN. PREHEAT THE OVEN TO 170°C/325°F/GAS 3. COVER THE CASSEROLE WITH A TIGHT-FITTING LID (YOU COULD USE A LAYER OF BAKING PARCHMENT BETWEEN THE LID AND CASSEROLE TO ENSURE A GOOD FIT.) COOK FOR ABOUT 1½ HOURS, OR UNTIL THE MEAT IS TENDER.

Variation
Chicken Tagine

Use the above recipe, omitting the lamb and using 5–6 partially boned chicken breasts with the skin still on instead *or* 1 medium/large chicken, divided into portions. When cooked, if partially boned chicken breasts have been used, trim away the bones from the back before reheating the breasts in the sauce and serving with couscous or rice.

Spicy Lamb Curry

Serves 5–6

This recipe is based on a traditional Malay curry. It's not a hot one, but it's full of interesting flavours. If you want to increase the spiciness, simply add more hot curry powder.

NOTE: THIS COULD ALSO BE MADE WITH PORK INSTEAD OF LAMB.

You will need:

1–1.2 kg (2¼–2½ lb) sliced shoulder of lamb or gigot chops (or lean pork cut into cubes)

2–3 tablespoons olive or vegetable oil

2–3 onions, sliced

2 cloves of garlic, chopped

1 heaped teaspoon hot curry powder

1 level teaspoon turmeric

2 level teaspoons coriander

1–2 level teaspoons cumin

5 cm (2 inch) piece of fresh ginger, peeled and chopped

3 whole cloves or ¼ teaspoon dried cloves

2 bay leaves

3 tomatoes, chopped

200 ml (7 fl oz) hot water or stock

salt and freshly ground black pepper

To serve:

rice, naan bread, chutney and poppadoms

1 Trim most of the fat off the meat and cut into generous sized pieces. If using gigot chops, there's no need to remove any bones until after cooking, not only because it will be easier then, but because the bones add flavour to the dish.

2 Heat the oil in a large heavy-based saucepan. Add the onion and garlic and fry to soften them, about 1–2 minutes. Add all the spices and heat gently for 1 minute, stirring to prevent any scorching. Add the lamb and stir well through the spicy mixture. Add the bay leaves, tomatoes, stock and seasoning. It may seem like there's not enough liquid, but the dish becomes more watery as it cooks.

3 Cover and simmer slowly for 1–1½ hours, until deliciously tender. You shouldn't have to thicken the juices or add more liquid. Serve with rice, naan bread, chutney and poppadoms.

Hot, Hot Goulash

Serves 5–6

A danger sign should be put on the labels of little jars of cayenne pepper. Try a tiny tip on your tongue and you'll see what I mean! Ground from cayenne chilli peppers, which are very hot, this popular spice has a reputation for helping poor circulation. Half a teaspoon should be enough here, but more can be used. However, don't be too enthusiastic when increasing it at the start or you may end up as I did – gasping for air!

This is one of my favourite comfort food recipes.

You will need:

700–900 g (1½–2 lb) stewing beef (a combination of rib and round steaks is good)

3–4 tablespoons olive oil

350–450 g (¾–1 lb) onions, sliced (about 3 medium onions)

2 cloves of garlic, chopped

2–3 rashers, chopped small

2–3 heaped teaspoons paprika (not a hot one)

½–¾ level teaspoon cayenne pepper or 3 teaspoons hot chilli powder

570 ml (1 pint) beef or chicken stock

1 x 400 g (14 oz) tin chopped tomatoes

2 teaspoons tomato purée

1 glass red wine (optional)

3–4 carrots, sliced

2 sticks celery, chopped

½–1 teaspoon herbes de Provence

salt and freshly ground black pepper

25 g (1 oz) each butter and flour (kneaded butter), to thicken (optional; see note on p.92)

To serve:

mashed potatoes

chopped fresh parsley

1 Cut the meat into bite-sized chunks, discarding all the fat and gristle.
2 Heat some of the oil in a pan and fry the meat in small batches, until browned all over. Transfer to a saucepan or casserole.
3 If liked, wipe out the pan and start again with fresh oil to fry the onions, garlic and the rashers for 2–3 minutes, until soft. Add the paprika and cayenne pepper and fry for a few seconds, then add the onion mixture to the meat. Pour the stock into the meat, adding

the tinned tomatoes, the tomato purée and the wine (if using). Add the carrots and celery and season well with the herbs, salt and pepper.

4 If using a saucepan, bring to the boil, then reduce the heat and simmer gently with the lid on for $1^1/_2$ hours, or until the meat is tender. If using a casserole, preheat the oven to 170°C/325°F/gas 3. When the oven is ready, cover the casserole with a well-fitting lid and cook in the oven for 2 hours, or until the meat is tender.

5 If you want to thicken the goulash juices, make the kneaded butter by mashing together the butter and flour to make a paste. Drop teaspoons of the paste into the steadily simmering stew, stirring briskly for a few minutes to cook the paste and thicken the juices.

6 Serve the goulash, scattered generously with chopped parsley, with mashed potatoes and a green vegetable of your choice.

Casserole Provençale

See photograph, page 93

Serves 5–6

Even in Provence in the south of France they have cold winters, and this richly flavoured casserole is native to the area. It has a lovely consistency after the long, slow cooking (ideally done in the oven, as that requires the least amount of attention). Of course, wine is an integral ingredient, which the lucky French can buy so cheaply. Don't hold back on the olives – they give a wonderful flavour to the finished dish. It's preferable to use fresh herbs rather than dried here.

You will need:

1 kg (2¼ lb) stewing beef, cut into generous bit-sized chunks

4 tablespoons olive oil

1 rounded tablespoon flour

200 g (7 oz) rashers, chopped (I like to use the smoked ones)

2 large onions, sliced

2 cloves of garlic, chopped

175 g (6 oz) button mushrooms, halved

2 large carrots, sliced

75–150 g (3–5 oz) black or green olives, stones removed

1 x 400 g (14 oz) tin chopped tomatoes

425 ml (¾ pint) hot beef stock

a little salt

plenty of freshly ground black pepper

For the marinade:

300 ml (½ pint) red wine

50 ml (2 fl oz) brandy (optional)

sprigs of fresh thyme

sprigs of fresh rosemary

2 bay leaves

2 cloves of garlic, chopped

a little salt

plenty of freshly ground black pepper

1   Put all the marinade ingredients into a bowl and stir well to combine. Add in the beef and mix well. Cover with clingfilm and allow to marinate in the fridge for a few hours. Stir once or twice if you think of it.

2   Preheat the oven to 170°C/325°F/gas 3.

3   Lift the meat out of the marinade with a slotted spoon (keep the marinade). Pat the meat dry with kitchen paper towels and fry in small batches until browned in the olive oil, then transfer to a casserole or heavy saucepan. Add the flour to the browned meat and toss together. Fry the rashers until golden and add to the meat.

4   Lightly brown the onions in the pan. Add the garlic and then the mushrooms, then add this mixture to the casserole. Put the carrots, olives and tinned tomatoes into the casserole.

5   Pour the marinade, including the herbs (but discard the rosemary – it's too pungent), into the pan the meat etc. was browned in and bring to the boil, making sure to scrape up all

the bits on the bottom of the pan. Boil for 1–2 minutes to reduce the amount of liquid a little and to intensify the flavour. Add the beef stock and simmer for a few minutes to heat it up, then pour the hot liquid directly into the casserole. The liquid should just about cover the meat and vegetables. Add very little salt, if any, because the rashers and olives are already salty. Add freshly ground black pepper and stir everything together. If necessary to make the lid fit more snugly, cover the casserole with a layer of baking parchment or tinfoil, then put on the lid (this helps to prevent evaporation).

6 Cook in the oven for $2^1/_2$–3 hours or until the meat is really tender. Discard the sprigs of fresh herbs before serving. Serve with mashed or boiled potatoes and a green vegetable of your choice.

Couscous Pilaf

Serves 4

This is a flavourful way to serve couscous, which is equally good hot or cold.

You will need:
2 tablespoons olive oil
1 small onion, chopped
1 small clove of garlic, chopped
225 g (8 oz) couscous
salt and freshly ground black pepper
300 ml ($^1/_2$ pint) chicken or vegetable stock

1 Heat the oil in a saucepan. Add the onion and garlic and cook for 1–2 minutes, until soft. Add the couscous, stir through and then pour in the stock. Season with salt and pepper.
2 Cover with a lid and cook gently for another few minutes, stirring occasionally, until heated through, then take off the heat and leave, covered, until the couscous swells, adding an extra drop of hot stock if necessary to keep it moist.
3 After about 5 minutes or so it should be ready to serve. Fluff up with a fork to break up any clumps.

Variation:

If serving couscous with other dishes, try including 75 g (3 oz) chopped mushrooms, 2–3 chopped tomatoes and a pinch of nutmeg in the above pilaf, adding them in at the start with the onions and garlic and frying for a few minutes.

CHAPTER 6

Meat

Minced Meat

It's often said that you can see the history of a country on its dinner plate. The local produce always dominates the dinner table, but its wars and victories, to say nothing of religions, all leave their mark on the national menu, such as in the form of a distinctive dish or a method of cooking that was adopted into the country's way of life.

Europeans' desire for spices led Columbus to set sail and discover a new world. He came back not only with gold, but with tomatoes, peppers, potatoes and more. Poor Columbus died in disgrace because he didn't achieve what he had set out to do – find an alternative route to the spice-growing countries in the Far East. In our little island off the west coast of Europe, which the Romans didn't even bother to conquer, we were unaware of the use of spices, so our cuisine used only local herbs and flavourings, such as parsley and thyme, without a hint of spice until relatively recently. Easy travel, television and now the influx of so many different nationalities have been creating a totally new look on our dinner plates. Walk inside any of the ethnic food stores now dotted around the country and discover an Aladdin's cave of spices and other unfamiliar ingredients.

Grilling and frying are quick methods of cooking, so tender cuts must be used. Naturally, one has to pay a little bit extra for that convenience.

Far from being the poor relation in a cook's repertoire of recipes, minced meat is the basis of many international dishes that include a wonderful diversity of ingredients used in different cultures. Different minced meats give their own individual flavour to the dishes.

Mincing meat is a time-honoured method of tenderising meat. Children tend to enjoy dishes using minced meat, as it's easy to chew. Once minced, meat also cooks more quickly.

NOTE: The process of mincing the meat creates a certain amount of heat and greatly increases the surface area of the meat. This makes it easier for bacteria to settle on the warm surface; therefore we are always advised to cook minced meat on the day of purchase. Once cooked, that danger is passed, as high heat kills most bacteria.

Minced Lamb Skewers (Lamb Keftas)

See photograph, p.103

Serves 3–4

The meat is well flavoured and then shaped into little sausage shapes in the palms of your hands.
Simply pierce each skewer right up the middle of the meat and squeeze tightly round it.

You will need:

450 g (1 lb) minced lamb

handful breadcrumbs

1 small egg, beaten

12–16 metal or bamboo skewers

For the spice and herb mixture:

1 teaspoon fennel seeds (optional)

1 teaspoon grated fresh ginger

1 teaspoon ground cumin

1 fresh red chilli, deseeded and finely chopped

2 cloves of garlic, chopped

salt and freshly ground black pepper

1 tablespoon chopped fresh coriander leaves

1 tablespoon chopped fresh mint leaves

2–3 tablespoons olive oil

To serve:

Tomato or mango salsa (see p.105)

**natural yoghurt mixed with chopped fresh mint, or fruit sauce and
  crème fraîche (see p.115)**

toasted pitta breads

NOTE: IF USING BAMBOO SKEWERS, THEY NEED TO BE WELL SOAKED IN WATER, PREFERABLY OVERNIGHT, ESPECIALLY IF YOU WILL BE USING THEM ON A BARBECUE. THIS PREVENTS THEM FROM CATCHING FIRE WHILE THE MEAT COOKS. SOAKING THEM FOR 30 MINUTES ISN'T REALLY ENOUGH.

---

1 Mix together all the ingredients for the spice and herb mixture using a pestle and mortar, a food processor or simply mix in a bowl with a wooden spoon. Add this mixture to the

minced lamb along with the breadcrumbs and egg and mix very well. The mixture must be fairly firm or it will fall off the skewers.

2   Using a rounded dessertspoon or tablespoon of the mixture at a time, form into sausage-like shapes in the palms of your hands and pierce the skewer right through the centre of the meat lengthways. Brush lightly with oil and place on a grill tray. Cook for 3–4 minutes on each side or until browned and cooked through. If the meat appears loose and is sticking to the grill, place a layer of oiled foil over the grill tray and put the keftas on the foil to cook.

3   Serve with tomato or mango salsa and some natural yoghurt served alongside. Toasted pitta bread also makes a good accompaniment.

NOTE: THESE CAN ALSO BE COOKED ON A BARBECUE.

Tomato or Mango Salsa

Makes 300–400 ml (10–14 fl oz)

If using mango, omit the tomatoes and use one ripe mango instead. Diced peaches or nectarines also make a good substitute for the mango. I keep a small bottle of Thai sweet chilli sauce in the fridge, as a spoonful or two added to any salsa gives a nice zing to the flavour.

You will need:
3 good red tomatoes, skinned (see note on p.43) or 1 large mango
$^1/_4$–$^1/_2$ small red pepper
10 cm (4 inch) piece of cucumber, peeled
$^1/_2$ small onion
salt and freshly ground black pepper
pinch cayenne pepper
1 tablespoon finely chopped fresh parsley
**1 tablespoon Thai sweet chilli sauce or 1–2 teaspoons sugar + 1–2
    teaspoons wine vinegar or lemon juice**

1   Cut the skinned tomatoes in half and scoop out the seeds and discard. Neatly chop the flesh. If using a mango, peel and then dice the flesh.

2   Neatly chop the pepper, cucumber and onion. Alternatively, you could put all the vegetables into a food processor and give them a short buzz to chop them even more finely. Season with salt and pepper and a hint of cayenne pepper, then stir in the parsley. Stir in the Thai sweet chilli sauce or add the sugar and lemon juice to taste.

Lamb Burgers with Goat's Cheese and Beetroot Salsa

Serves 4–5

The concept of a small cake of minced beef is an old one, but the particular version that we know as the hamburger originated in the Baltic area. It seems that this was adopted by the seamen of Hamburg as a convenient package of meat, and it travelled with them when they emigrated to the US. In 1904, the hamburger was a feature at the St Louis World's Fair, where it was devoured by droves of visitors and so acquired a new status.

Much unpleasant food has masqueraded under the name of a burger, but a homemade burger is hard to beat. Making them yourself means you have control over the ingredients. Simple to prepare, the range of variations is considerable.

Buy the vacuum-packed cooked beetroots (not the jars of beetroot in vinegar) for the beetroot salsa, which contrasts excellently with the goat's cheese topping.

NOTE: THESE BURGERS CAN ALSO BE MADE WITH BEEF.

NOTE: FETA CHEESE CAN BE USED INSTEAD OF GOAT'S CHEESE.

You will need:
500–700g (1¼–1½ lb) good-quality lean lamb (or beef), minced
1 small/medium onion, finely chopped
1–2 cloves of garlic, crushed (optional)
a little olive oil for frying
salt and freshly ground black pepper
1 teaspoon ground cumin
¼ teaspoon dried oregano or thyme
1 tablespoon of finely chopped fresh parsley leaves
½ tablespoon of finely chopped fresh mint leaves (omit if you are using beef)

For the beetroot salsa:
250 g (9 oz) vacuum-packed cooked beetroot
small handful of fresh coriander leaves, chopped (optional)
1–2 tablespoons redcurrant jelly or blackcurrant jam
salt and freshly ground black pepper

To serve:
110–150 g (4–5 oz) goat's cheese (or feta cheese)
4 burger buns, split and toasted on the cut side
salad leaves

1 Place the minced lamb in a bowl. Fry the onion and garlic in about 1 tablespoon of olive oil for 1–2 minutes, until soft, then add to the meat, including the oil. Add the other ingredients to the meat. Mix well and shape into 4–5 round burgers (not too thick, or they will take too long to cook in the centre). Set aside while you prepare the beetroot salsa.

2 To make the salsa, dice the beetroot very small (or buzz in a food processor) and put into a bowl. Add the coriander leaves if using and redcurrant jelly to taste. Season with salt and pepper.

3 Grill or fry the burgers for about 5–6 minutes per side or until done to your liking. Slice or crumble the goat's cheese or feta on top and place under a grill to warm through (it won't brown very successfully).

4 Serve the burgers on the toasted buns on top of the lettuce leaves and with the beetroot salsa spooned on top, with any extra served in a bowl alongside.

Meatloaf

I can fully understand the popularity of meatloaf in America. Easy to make, inexpensive and highly versatile, a meatloaf can be served hot from the oven or cold with salads or in sandwiches. There are multiple variations of the basic recipe for meatloaf. I'm partial to including a little tomato ketchup in the mix for the delicate punch it gives to the flavour.

You will need:

750 g (1¹/₂ lb) good-quality minced beef

1 large onion, finely chopped

1–2 fat cloves of garlic

2–3 tablespoons olive oil

150 g (5 oz) back or streaky rashers, finely chopped

150 g (5 oz) mushrooms, finely chopped

salt and freshly ground black pepper

75 g (3 oz) breadcrumbs

¹/₂ teaspoon dried oregano

¹/₄ teaspoon dried thyme

2 tablespoons chopped fresh parsley

1 large egg, beaten lightly

2 tablespoons tomato ketchup

generous pinch (or more) ground nutmeg

a little extra olive oil for brushing the meatloaf

For the gravy:

2 tablespoons olive oil

reserved spoonfuls of rashers and mushroom from the meatloaf

40 g (1¹/₂ oz) flour

425–570 ml (3/4–1 pint) beef stock

salt and freshly ground black pepper

1 dessertspoon Worcestershire sauce

1 dessertspoon tomato ketchup or redcurrant jelly

1 Preheat the oven to 200°C/400°F/gas 6.
2 Put the minced meat into a bowl. Fry the onion and garlic in some of the olive oil for 1–2 minutes, until soft. Add the chopped rashers and fry, stirring frequently, until they change colour. Set aside 1–2 tablespoons of this mixture in a small bowl for adding to the gravy later and add all the rest to the minced meat in the bowl.
3 Fry the chopped mushrooms in the pan, adding a little extra oil if necessary, for 2–3

minutes, until soft. Season with salt and pepper. Set aside 1 tablespoon of these mushrooms for the gravy, adding all the remaining mushrooms to the meat in the bowl. Stir all the remaining ingredients into the minced meat and mix thoroughly.

4   Put a large piece of foil, shiny side up, on a roasting tin and brush the centre with oil. Shape the meatloaf into a rectangle about 5–7.5 cm (2–3 inches) high and place in the centre of the foil. Brush the top with a little oil and place the tin in the oven (foil still opened out) and cook for 15–20 minutes to set the loaf and lightly brown the outside.

5   Remove from the oven and draw the edges of the foil over to cover the meatloaf. Continue cooking for 30–40 minutes more, or until cooked through. The foil may be opened out for the final 10 minutes of cooking to crisp the outside if desired. If serving hot, transfer to a hot plate and leave to stand for about 10 minutes to rest before slicing.

6   To make the gravy while the meatloaf cooks, heat the olive oil in a pan. Stir in the flour to make a coarse paste. Cook gently to turn the paste a light golden brown colour without burning. Gradually stir in the stock and the remaining ingredients. Add the reserved tablespoons of fried onion, rashers and mushrooms. Bring to the boil and simmer gently for a few minutes. Cover and leave to one side until ready to serve, then reheat again.

NOTE: AFTER LIFTING THE COOKED MEATLOAF OUT OF THE TIN, IF THERE ARE ANY NICE TASTY BITS LEFT IN THE TIN, POUR IN SOME OF THE GRAVY YOU HAVE MADE AND STIR IT AROUND TO GATHER THEM ALL UP. IF THE GRAVY HAS NOT YET BEEN MADE, SIMPLY POUR IN SOME OF THE STOCK AND DO LIKEWISE, THEN USE IT TO MAKE THE GRAVY.

Swedish Meatballs with Honey Mustard Sauce

Serves 3

These flavoursome meatballs can be served with spaghetti or with mashed potatoes.

You will need:

350 g (12 oz) lean minced steak

110 g (4 oz) back rashers, chopped finely

25 g (1 oz) butter

1 tablespoonful sunflower or olive oil

1 onion, finely chopped

1 clove of garlic, chopped

40g (1½ oz) breadcrumbs

1 egg, beaten

salt and freshly ground black pepper

1–2 teaspoonfuls grated fresh ginger

pinch nutmeg

1 teaspoon Dijon mustard

sunflower oil, for frying

For the honey mustard sauce:

any tasty little bits left after frying the meatballs (oil drained off)

1 tablespoon honey

2 teaspoons wholegrain mustard

400 ml (14 fl oz) chicken or vegetable stock

3 tablespoons crème fraîche (optional but good!)

4 spring onions, thinly sliced

½ small red chilli, very thinly sliced (optional)

1   Put the mince and rashers into a bowl. Heat the butter and oil and fry the onion and garlic together for 1–2 minutes, until soft. Add to the meats with all the other ingredients. Mix everything well together.

2   Using a dessertspoon as a measure, form the meat mixture into little balls. Heat plenty of the sunflower oil in a pan and lightly fry the meatballs until cooked through and browned on the outside.

NOTE: THESE CAN BE COOKED COMPLETELY IN THE PAN, OR IF PREFERRED, THEY CAN BE FINISHED OFF IN THE OVEN. PLACE THEM SIDE BY SIDE (WITH SPACE BETWEEN) ON A BAKING TIN AND BAKE THEM IN A HOT OVEN (PREHEATED TO 200°C/400°F/GAS 6) FOR 20 MINUTES, UNTIL COOKED THROUGH.

3   To make the honey mustard sauce, add all the sauce ingredients to the pan and bring to the boil. (The sauce can be thickened slightly by adding 1 heaped teaspoon of cornflour, mixed to a paste with a little cold water. Bring to the boil, stirring, until thickened.) Season with salt and pepper.

4   Transfer the meatballs into the honey mustard sauce and serve on spaghetti or mashed potatoes. Accompany with a tossed salad.

Turkish Lamb Pittas

Serves 4

This is a tasty, quick snack or lunch.

You will need:

salt and freshly ground black pepper

$^1/_2$ teaspoon ground cumin

$^1/_2$ teaspoon ground coriander

550–700 g (1$^1/_4$–1$^1/_2$ lb) lean, tender lamb

2–4 tablespoons olive oil

25 g (1 oz) pine nuts

1 medium onion, chopped

1–2 cloves of garlic, chopped

450 g (1 lb) tomatoes, skinned and chopped (see note on p.43)

To serve:

225 g (8 oz) Greek-style yoghurt

2–4 oval shaped wholemeal pitta breads (see note)

NOTE: USE ONE WHOLE TOASTED PITTA PER SERVING, OR IF PREFERRED, SLIT THE PITTA BREAD IN TWO AND USE ONLY ONE HALF PER SERVING.

---

1   Mix together the salt, pepper and spices. Cut the lamb into thin bite-sized strips and toss in the spice mixture. Set aside.
2   Heat a little oil in a frying pan over a moderate heat and sauté the pine nuts until golden, taking care not to burn them. Lift out with a slotted spoon and set aside.
3   Add more oil to the pan and fry the onion and garlic for 1–2 minutes, until soft. Add the tomatoes and fry until they're tender but not mushy. Season the mixture with salt and pepper, then lift out and keep warm.
4   Add the remaining olive oil to the pan and increase the heat. When it's really hot, add the lamb a few pieces at a time and cook quickly until they're nicely browned.
5   To assemble, place a pitta bread on each plate. Spoon the tomato and onion mixture on top of the pitta, then arrange the pieces of lamb on top of that. Gently heat the yoghurt until just warm, either in the frying pan or in the microwave and spoon as generously as you like over the lamb. Scatter the pine nuts on top.

NOTE: IF PREFERRED, THE COOKED INGREDIENTS CAN BE SERVED INSIDE THE PITTAS, IN WHICH CASE THIS MAKES ENOUGH TO FILL UP TO SIX PITTA BREADS.

Marinated Lamb Chops with Fruit Sauce

Serves 6

Marinades can give great depth of flavour to most foods and they're a fun way to try out different combinations of flavours. A marinade can also have a tenderising effect on meat. The amount of marinade in this recipe is just enough to smear over the chops.

You will need:

6 lamb chops

For the marinade:

2 teaspoons paprika

1 teaspoon ground cumin

1 thin finger-length red chilli, finely chopped

1–2 cloves of garlic, crushed

1 tablespoon fresh mint, chopped

6 tablespoons olive oil

salt and freshly ground black pepper

For the fruit sauce:

200 g (7 oz) crème fraîche

1 nectarine (or ½ ripe mango), peeled and coarsely grated

1 tablespoon chopped chives

1 tablespoon mango chutney

4–5 leaves of fresh mint, chopped finely

salt and freshly ground black pepper

1 Mix together all the ingredients for the marinade. Put the chops in a single layer in a dish and spread the marinade all over the chops on both sides. Cover and put into the fridge for an hour. After 30 minutes, turn the chops over in the marinade.

2 To cook, lift out of the marinade and brush off any excess. Grill the chops, allowing about 6 minutes for each side or until cooked to your liking. If preferred, bake the chops on a flat tin in a hot oven (200°C/400°F/gas 6) for about 30 minutes or cook on the barbecue.

3 To make the fruit sauce, simply mix all the ingredients together.

4 Serve the chops with the fruit sauce. Accompany with baked potatoes, a tossed salad and/or coleslaw.

Fillet of Steak (Tournedos)

Serves 2

Tournedos is the name the French give to the compact round steaks cut from the centre, or eye, of the fillet or closer to the narrow end. Fried or grilled, the tournedos are delicious served on individual rounds of fried bread. In my version of this recipe, the rounds of fried bread are spread with a layer of duck liver pâté, with the fried tournedos placed on top. A simple sauce made with a splash of brandy or whiskey, cream and a little wholegrain mustard is the finishing touch.

You will need:

2 slices of fillet steak (tournedos), about 175 g (6 oz) each, trimmed of any fat and sinew

freshly ground black pepper

1 small onion, thinly sliced

$^1/_4$–$^1/_2$ small clove of garlic, sliced

4–5 button mushrooms, thinly sliced

2–3 tablespoons olive oil

2–3 heaped teaspoons butter

salt

2 circles white bread, large enough to fit under the slices of fillet steak (note that the steak will shrink a little during cooking)

2 heaped teaspoons duck liver pâté (or any other pâté of your choice)

2 tablespoons brandy

175 ml (6 fl oz) cream

$^1/_4$–$^1/_2$ teaspoon wholegrain mustard

1. Take the steaks out of the fridge 30 minutes or so before required to bring them to room temperature. Season lightly with freshly ground black pepper.
2. Fry the onion, garlic and mushrooms in a little of the olive oil and butter for 2–4 minutes, until soft. Season with salt and pepper. Lift out and keep warm.
3. In the same pan, adding more oil and butter if necessary, fry the bread until golden on both sides. (If you're watching calories, you might prefer to toast the bread instead of frying it, though it won't be as tasty!) Spread thickly with the pâté and keep warm.
4. When ready to serve, heat some more olive oil and butter in the pan and fry the steaks on both sides to brown them, making sure to brown the thick edges of the steaks as well (hold the steaks sideways with tongs to do this). Continue to fry for 3–5 minutes per side, depending on the thickness, until well browned but still rare (pink and moist) in the middle. Increase the cooking time if you like your steak well done. Take out of the pan and keep warm while you quickly make the sauce.
5. Spoon any excess fat off the pan, add the brandy and cook briskly to reduce by a third.

Pour in the cream, season lightly with salt and pepper and stir in the mustard. Bring just barely to the boil.

6 Place the circles of fried bread in the centre of warm dinner plates. Sit the tournedos on top, spooning a little of the mushroom and onion mixture on top of each and then spoon the sauce over. Serve immediately.

Chunky Chilli Wraps

Serves 2–3

Because this dish cooks quickly, it's important to buy tender steak. The flour tortillas provide the starch element of the dish instead of the more usual potatoes or rice. A tossed salad served with this provides the vitamins required from fresh vegetables.

You will need:

1–2 tablespoons olive or corn oil

350 g (12 oz) sirloin steak, cut into strips

1 small onion (red if liked), chopped

1–2 cloves of garlic, chopped

1 medium red pepper, deseeded and chopped

2 mild green chillies, seeded and roughly chopped

1¹/₂–1 level teaspoon ground cumin

¹/₂ teaspoon hot chilli powder

salt and freshly ground black pepper

¹/₂ x 400 g (14 oz) tin chopped tomatoes

¹/₂ x 400 g (14 oz) tin red kidney beans, drained and rinsed

1–2 teaspoons Worcestershire sauce

To serve:

4–6 flour tortillas

fromage frais or Greek-style yoghurt

1 Heat the tortillas by placing them on a plate and covering with a damp paper kitchen towel. Heat in the microwave for 30–60 seconds or more (or see note). Keep warm while you make the filling.

NOTE: MY TOASTER IS THE IDEAL GADGET IN WHICH TO HEAT THE TORTILLAS BECAUSE IT HAS ONE LONG OPENING RATHER THAN TWO SLOTS. I JUST DROP THE FOLDED TORTILLA, FOLD SIDE DOWNWARDS, INTO THE TOASTER AND TOAST UNTIL HOT AND VERY SLIGHTLY GOLDEN. ANOTHER METHOD IS TO FRY THE TORTILLAS ONE AT A TIME AND ON ONE SIDE ONLY FOR A FEW SECONDS IN A LIGHTLY OILED PAN. THIS MAKES THEM DELIGHTFULLY CRISPY ON THE FRIED SIDE. (IF MAKING THEM THIS WAY, PUT THE FILLING ON THE UNFRIED SIDE AND FOLD OVER.)

2 Heat some of the oil in a large frying pan (or wok). Add half the beef and fry for 2–3 minutes, until browned. Remove with a slotted spoon and set aside on a plate. Repeat with the remaining beef, adding a drizzle more oil if required. If liked, partially wipe out some of the dark sediment left by the meat in the pan.

3 Add the onion, garlic, red pepper and green chillies along with a little drizzle of oil. Fry over a moderate heat to soften the vegetables a little. Add the cumin, chilli powder, salt and pepper. Depending on personal taste, you can increase the hot chilli powder, but do so cautiously! Stir in the tomatoes and the beans. Add the Worcestershire sauce and add the fried meat back into the pan.

4 Cover the pan and cook for a few minutes, until the sauce begins to bubble. Continue to cook gently for about 5 minutes.

5 Serve the meat in the heated tortillas. Put a generous spoonful of fromage frais on each serving and accompany with a salad or coleslaw.

Honeyed Pork Kebabs

Serves 3–4

This marinade gives a good flavour to the pork. You could also use lamb. This is ideal for a barbecue. Serve with baked potatoes and a salad.

You will need:

450 g (1 lb) lean pork (or lamb), cut into 2.5 cm (1 inch) cubes (see note)

juice of 1 orange

1 tablespoon balsamic vinegar

1 tablespoon honey

4 tablespoons olive oil

salt and freshly ground pepper

sprig of fresh rosemary

sprig of fresh thyme

$\frac{1}{2}$ onion, chopped

1 clove of garlic, crushed or chopped

4 metal or bamboo skewers (see note)

NOTE: STEEP BAMBOO SKEWERS IN WATER FOR AT LEAST 1–2 HOURS TO PREVENT THEM BURNING, ESPECIALLY ON A BARBECUE.

1   Trim any fat or gristle from the meat. Put all the remaining ingredients, including the fresh herbs, in a bowl and mix well. Add the meat and stir to coat. Cover the bowl and leave for at least 1 hour (or it can be left overnight), stirring occasionally.

2   Thread the meat onto the skewers, brush with oil and grill until browned on all sides. Serve.

NOTE: FOR A CHANGE, BUY A PORK STEAK AND CUT IT INTO THREE EVEN LENGTHS. SLIT EACH LENGTH RIGHT DOWN THE CENTRE IF THE STEAK IS THICK ENOUGH, MAKING IT INTO 'FINGERS'. STEEP IN THE ABOVE MARINADE AND THEN PIERCE A SKEWER RIGHT UP THROUGH THE CENTRE OF EACH 'FINGER' OF PORK AND GRILL.

CHAPTER 7

Roasts

In times long gone, roasting meat was done on a turning spit in front of a big open fire with a pan underneath to catch the melting fat, as the meat required nearly continuous basting to prevent it drying out. Roasting meat in an oven is much easier and requires little basting. A meat thermometer is a handy gadget to help judge when the meat is cooked as required.

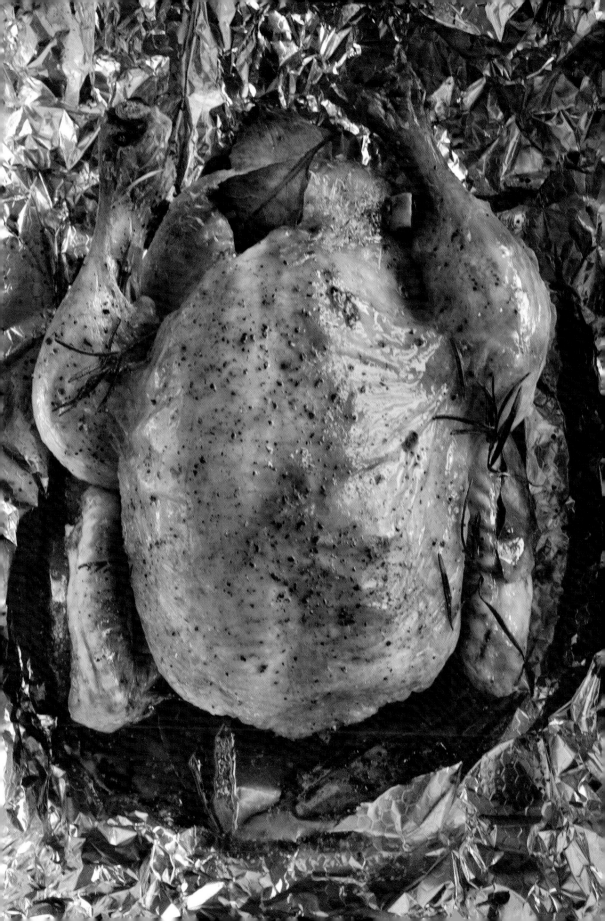

Herb, Lemon and Garlic Roast Chicken

See photograph, p.123

Serves 4–5

The wonderful aroma that fills the kitchen when you take a roast chicken out of the oven is enough to bring the whole family running. Plainly roasted with some garlic, lemon and herbs, a chicken is undemanding of the cook, yet it will emerge from the oven tantalisingly tender and moist, covered with crispy golden skin. Buy the best quality that you can manage, trying different brands or butchers until you find a nice firm-fleshed chicken. Free-range or even organic chickens are good. You will pay a bit more, but it should be worth it.

In contrast to roast beef or lamb, which can be served rare (underdone), chicken should be well cooked right through. I prefer to remove any string or skewers that bunch the chicken legs into the body, allowing them to sit loosely so that the heat penetrates more easily.

To prevent the chicken drying out during roasting, I like to sit it on a large piece of tinfoil, large enough to fold up and cover it completely. I find this keeps the flesh moist. Then, at the end of the cooking time, open the foil and allow the skin to brown deliciously. As an interesting titbit, the innovative chef Heston Blumenthal (chef patron of the Fat Duck Restaurant in Bray, Berkshire, complete with his three Michelin stars) likes to cook a plain roast chicken for his family Sunday lunch. He uses a very low oven temperature and the chicken takes about 5 hours to cook! He also recommends using a meat thermometer when roasting meats because ovens vary so much.

You will need:

1 large chicken (1.8 kg/4 lb)

olive oil

sprigs of fresh thyme and parsley and a bay leaf (or dried herbes de Provence)

3–4 cloves of garlic, halved and chopped (no need to remove the skins)

1 lemon, halved

coarse sea salt and freshly ground black pepper

To serve:

gravy (see p.125)

1 Preheat the oven to 200°C/400°F/gas 6. After about 40 minutes, the oven can be reduced to 190°C/375°F/gas 5.
2 Remove the bag of giblets (if there are any) from inside the cavity of the chicken.

Remove any elastic bands or string and leave the legs loose. Place the tin foil (shiny side up) on a roasting tin and drizzle a little olive oil in the base, then sit the chicken on top of the oiled foil. Tuck little sprigs of herbs and chopped garlic wherever they will fit around the chicken or sprinkle sparingly with dried herbs.

3 Squeeze the juice from half the lemon over the top of the chicken, then cut up the squeezed-out lemon rind and tuck it around the chicken. Put the other lemon half into the body cavity, along with a few small sprigs of herbs and a clove of garlic. Season the chicken generously with salt and pepper. Drizzle olive oil all over the chicken. Fold the foil over the chicken to cover it completely and so keep the moisture inside.

4 Chicken should be served well cooked, not pink and underdone. I recommend about 30 minutes' roasting time per 450 g (1 lb) chicken weight plus an extra 30 minutes at the end (and allow an extra bit of time for resting after roasting). These roasting times apply to a chicken that is at room temperature and not cold from the fridge – otherwise allow longer. I'm always anxious that the chicken be well cooked, so I like to start roasting even a little earlier than the calculations would suggest, as a cooked chicken will wait for you (covered with the cooking foil and a clean tea towel).

5 About 20 minutes before the end of the roasting time, turn back the foil and allow the chicken to brown. When the foil is opened out, carefully tilt the roasting tin (holding the chicken with oven gloves to prevent it slipping out) and pour off any juices and fat to prevent them evaporating during the browning process. Leave to one side to let the fat rise to the top. To check if the chicken is cooked, pull the leg out from the body and cut the skin to see if the flesh around the bones is well cooked and not still pink and raw looking. If it's still pink, cook longer.

6 Let the chicken stand, covered, for 10 minutes before carving while you make the gravy. Remove the fat from the pan juices and store in the fridge to use when preparing your next soup or stew. Add the remaining juices to the gravy.

Gravy

Lift the chicken out of the roasting tin, pour about 425 ml (³/₄ pint) boiling water into the foil in the roasting tin and stir to gather up all the tasty bits left behind. Crumble a chicken stock cube into it if you like. In a separate saucepan, melt 2–3 tablespoons of the chicken fat (or butter). Add 2–3 tablespoons of flour and mix to a paste, cooking until golden. Stir in the chicken stock (strained if necessary) and add some of the juices from the chicken (underneath the chicken fat in the bowl). Bring to the boil. Season if necessary with salt and pepper and add 1 tablespoon of redcurrant jelly.

Cheat's Gravy

I often cheat when making gravy, using a favourite packet of gravy mix or even combining two different types. When made, I add the juices from the roasted chicken (fat spooned off). A spoonful of redcurrant jelly is also rather nice. Just add it in and bring to the boil before serving.

Butterflied Leg of Lamb

Serves 6

Originally from America, this recipe removes the bone from a leg of lamb, and instead of rolling it up again, the meat is laid out flat, at which point it's described as looking like a butterfly. The butcher will remove the bone for you (though in fact it's not too difficult if you have a sharp knife).

Covered with herbs and flavourings before cooking, the resulting flavour is delicious and a dream to carve. Place the boned-out leg, opened out and skin side downwards, on the roasting tin. The raw surface of the joint will be lumpy and uneven. Some of these lumps will cook at different rates, which means there will be a choice of well done and pink lamb. Alternatively, you can roast the lamb with the skin side facing up.

Young spring lamb will cook quite quickly, especially if you like to serve it pink. This joint could be cooked on a barbecue. I prefer to roast it in the oven, though if need be, I'll do the final browning on the barbecue. For an older lamb, the cooking time will be longer.

NOTE: LAMB CAN BE COOKED LEAN SIDE UP (AS IN THE PHOTO) OR TURNED OVER SO THAT THE SKIN SIDE IS UPPERMOST.

You will need:
1 butterflied leg of lamb (weigh the meat)
a few sprigs of fresh rosemary
¹/₂ teaspoondried oregano

For the marinade:
4 tablespoons olive oil
1–2 tablespoons balsamic vinegar
juice and grated rind of ¹/₂ lemon
¹/₂ teaspoon French mustard
2–4 cloves of garlic, crushed
salt and freshly ground black pepper

1 If your roasting tin isn't wide enough for the butterflied leg to lie flat, simply use a baking tin. Mix all the marinade ingredients together and spoon it all over the surface of the meat. Scatter small sprigs of rosemary over and under the meat and sprinkle on the oregano. Cover the tin with foil and leave for at least 1 hour or longer.

2 Preheat the oven to 200°C/400°F/gas 6. Cook the lamb for about 1 ¹/₂ hours (about 15 minutes for every 450 g (1 lb) of meat (off the bone), plus an extra 15 minutes of cooking at the end). Alternatively, you can roast at a lower temperature

(180°C/350°F/gas 4), allowing about 25 minutes per 450 g (1 lb) plus an extra 25 minutes at the end, after removing the foil. Baste occasionally during cooking.

3 If you want the lamb pink, check when you think it's done by piercing the thickest part with a skewer, holding a tablespoon just underneath to catch the escaping juices, which should be pink. Cook longer if you prefer it well done (until the juices are golden). For the last 20 minutes of cooking, remove the foil to allow the lamb to brown, or simply transfer the meat to the barbecue.

Variation: A spicy marinade

You will need:

1–2 long, thin red chillies, finely chopped

4 cloves of garlic, crushed

1 teaspoon cumin

$^1/_2$ teaspoon paprika

salt and freshly ground black pepper

handful of coriander, chopped

finely grated zest of $^1/_2$ lemon

4 tablespoons olive oil

1 tablespoon lemon juice

Pork Belly

Serves about 4

Deliciously tasty, a simple pork belly has the extra bonus of crispy, crackling skin to munch on.
If you can choose the thicker end of the cut, you will get the leaner joint suitable for roasting. For
genuinely crisp crackling, ask your butcher to score the skin in thin, narrow lines. You could do it
yourself with a Stanley knife, but the skin is very tough. Be sure the skin is dry (not wet from a vacuum
pack or just defrosted). Ignore advice about rubbing the skin with oil or any other fat, as it prevents a
really good crackling finish. Simply mix together some seasonings and dried mixed herbs, maybe even a
hint of nutmeg, and rub this mixture over the skin and down into the cuts.

You will need:

**1.4–1.8 kg (3–4 lb) belly of pork, with the skin on and the bones
   removed**

¹/₂ teaspoon salt

¹/₂ teaspoon freshly ground black pepper

generous pinches of mixed herbs or oregano or fresh thyme leaves

a few pinches of ground nutmeg or fennel seeds

For the bed of vegetables:

¹/₂ Bramley cooking apple, sliced

1 large onion, peeled and sliced

1 potato, sliced

1 stick of celery, sliced

1–2 cloves of garlic, chopped

1–2 small sprigs of fresh thyme and/or 2 fresh bay leaves

600 ml (1 pint) light chicken stock or water

For the gravy:

300 ml (¹/₂ pint) chicken stock

salt and freshly ground black pepper

¹/₂ teaspoon mustard

25 g (1 oz) butter

25 g (1 oz) flour

1 Preheat the oven to 230°C/450°F/gas 8.

2 Allow the meat to come to room temperature before starting to cook it – it should not be cold from the fridge. Mix the seasoning, herbs and nutmeg together and rub into the surface of the skin, especially into the cuts.

3 Arrange a bed of sliced vegetables in a thick layer in the middle of a roasting tin to fit under the meat. Scatter the garlic over and season with salt and pepper. Place the sprigs of thyme and/or bay leaves on the vegetables and sit the meat on top. Pour the stock or water into the tin around the vegetables to keep the meat moist.

4 Place in the oven and roast, uncovered, for 25–30 minutes, then reduce the heat to 190°C/375°F/gas 5 and continue to cook, allowing 25–30 minutes of cooking time for every 450 g (1 lb) meat (see note).

5 When cooked to your liking (you can cut into the roast to check if the meat is cooked if necessary), lift out of the roasting tin onto a warm plate and keep warm for about 15 minutes before serving.

6 Meanwhile, make the gravy. Add the stock, seasoning and mustard into the vegetables and juices left in the tin and bring gently to the boil on the top of the cooker. Pour through a sieve, taste for seasoning if necessary and reheat. Mash the butter and flour together with a fork to make kneaded butter, then thicken the gravy with enough of the kneaded butter, stirred in little bits into the briskly simmering juices, to thicken to your liking. Serve with the meat.

NOTE: AFTER THE INITIAL 25 MINUTES OF HIGH HEAT, THE OVEN TEMPERATURE CAN BE LOWERED TO 180°C/350°F/GAS 4, ALLOWING ABOUT 45 MINUTES OF COOKING TIME FOR EVERY 450 G (1 LB) MEAT.

Roast Duck

Serves 2–4, depending on appetite!

Many recipes suggest first pouring boiling water from a kettle over the whole duck before roasting it, thoroughly patting the skin dry and even letting it stand for a few hours in a cool, dry place. This is to ensure a crisp skin. Then prick the duck skin here and there with a sharp knife to help release the melting fat. I suggest piercing these little holes not on top of the breast, but rather lower down, closer to the wings and legs.

You will need:
1.8 kg (4 lb) duck
3 cloves of garlic
sprigs of fresh thyme and parsley

1 Preheat the oven to 200°C/400°F/gas 6.
2 Ideally, sit the duck on a wire tray in a roasting tin so the fat can drip down. Insert some garlic and herbs into the body cavity. Allow about 55 minutes of roasting time per 1 kg (2 lb). After the first 40 minutes of roasting, you can lift out the roasting tin and pour off the fat that will have gathered in the tin to save for another use (see note).
3 When cooked, pierce the leg with a skewer – if the juices are pink, return it to the oven for another 5–10 minutes and test again.

NOTE: IF YOU WISH TO KEEP THE FAT (AND YOU SHOULD – IT ADDS GREAT FLAVOUR TO ROAST POTATOES AND OTHER VEGETABLES AND CAN BE USED TO MAKE THE CONFIT OF DUCK ON P.132), DON'T BRUSH ANY GLAZE ON THE DUCK UNTIL AFTER YOU'VE SAVED SOME OF THE MELTED FAT, OTHERWISE THE MELTED FAT WILL HAVE OTHER UNNECESSARY FLAVOURS IN IT.

Confit of Duck with Puy Lentils

Serves 4

On holidays in Napa Valley, California some years ago, we stopped in Yountville, a smart little town in the centre of the wine-growing area. We had lunch at an elegant bistro-style restaurant, and though the name escapes me, I can still remember the confit of duck that I ate, served with Puy lentils.

It's actually quite easy to make confit of duck. All you need is plenty of duck fat or even goose fat, ideally left over after you've roasted a duck (see p.131). The recipe is a classic French way of cooking and preserving joints of duck (and some other meats). The cooked portions of duck can be eaten straight away or stored in a dish covered with the cooking fat, where they will keep for a few weeks in a fridge. First, the duck portions are seasoned and flavoured with herbs and left, covered, overnight. The next day they are cooked slowly in duck fat until the meat is melt-in-the-mouth tender.

To serve, melt the fat off the portions and crisp in a hot oven. If serving straight away, you don't need as much fat as is required when covering them for preserving. Confit of duck can be served as a light lunch dish or as a starter.

You will need:

For the duck confit:

4 duck legs or 2 legs and 2 breasts

coarse sea salt and freshly ground black pepper

1 clove of garlic, chopped

sprig of rosemary

small knob of fresh ginger, thinly sliced

piece of orange peel (white pith removed)

400 ml (14 fl oz) duck fat

For the lentils:

175 g (6 oz) Puy lentils

1 tablespoon olive oil

1 tablespoon finely chopped onion

1 small clove of garlic, crushed

1–2 teaspoons finely chopped red chilli, seeds discarded (optional)

vegetable stock (see note)

white wine (optional; see note)

salt and freshly ground black pepper

small knob of butter

a drizzle of fresh lemon juice or balsamic vinegar

1 To make the confit, rub salt and pepper into the skin and flesh of the duck portions and place, skin side down, on a plate. Scatter the garlic, rosemary, ginger and orange peel over the meat. Cover with cling film and store in the fridge for 12–24 hours.

2 Empty the duck fat into a saucepan that's just large enough for the portions to sit side by side and heat to simmering. Put the duck portions along with all the herbs and bits and pieces into the fat. Bring to the boil, then reduce the heat right down and simmer very

gently for 1–1$^{1}/_{2}$ hours, or until the meat is really tender. Turn occasionally. Lift out and set aside to cool.

3 When cool, pack the duck into a clean container (that has been scalded with boiling water to ensure cleanliness). Strain the fat through a sieve and leave to stand in a bowl to allow any meat juices to sink to the bottom. Only use the fat on top. Pour this fat over the cooked duck to cover it completely. Ideally, leave the confit for a few days to mature.

4 To reheat, scrape the loose fat off the duck portions and cook on a pan or in a hot oven to melt off the remaining fat. Heat the portions until the duck is piping hot and the skin is crisp.

5 To prepare the lentils, first put them into a sieve and rinse under cold water.

6 Heat the olive oil in a small saucepan. Add the onion, garlic and chilli and cook gently for 1–2 minutes to soften. Add the washed lentils and the stock (and wine if using it). Season with salt and pepper.

7 Bring to the boil, then simmer for 15–20 minutes, until the lentils are soft but not mushy. Strain off the excess liquid. Add the knob of butter and some lemon juice or balsamic vinegar to taste. Season again with salt and pepper if necessary.

NOTE: PUY LENTILS, GROWN IN FRANCE, ARE A DARK GREEN, ALMOST SLATE-GREY COLOUR AND ARE VALUED FOR THEIR EARTHY FLAVOUR. COOKING THEM IN STOCK OR A COMBINATION OF STOCK AND WHITE WINE GIVES THEM EXTRA FLAVOUR. MEASURE THE VOLUME OF THE LENTILS IN A MEASURING JUG, THEN USE TWICE THAT VOLUME OF STOCK (OR A COMBINATION OF STOCK AND WHITE WINE).

Roast Shoulder of Lamb

Serves 6–8

Less expensive than the leg, a shoulder of lamb has a sweet flavour. The downside is that the meat is difficult to carve and there are fatty bits. Try roasting the whole shoulder until it's so tender it almost comes off the bone. (Bones add good flavour to all roasts.)

You will need:
1 whole shoulder of lamb
sprigs of rosemary
3 cloves of garlic
$^1\!/_2$ teaspoon thyme
$^1\!/_2$ teaspoon oregano
salt and freshly ground black pepper

For the gravy:
1–2 teaspoons flour
150 ml ($^1\!/_4$ pint) wine (boil to reduce by a third)
150 ml ($^1\!/_4$ pint) stock
1–2 teaspoons redcurrant jelly

1 Preheat the oven to 170°C/325°F/gas 3.
2 Using a sharp knife, cut shallow slits in the fat on the lamb and insert a tiny sprig of rosemary or piece of garlic into each slit. Alternatively, crush the garlic, mix with the herbs and rub all over the surface of the lamb. Season with salt and pepper and drizzle a little olive oil over the surface of the meat. Sit the joint on a rack in the roasting tin with the sprigs of rosemary tucked underneath or sit on a little mound of vegetables just underneath the meat (such as some sliced onion, carrots, celery and potato, seasoned with salt and pepper and some of the herbs).
3 Place in the oven and roast gently for at least 2 hours or longer, as you like. When it gets brown enough on top, cover it loosely with foil. When cooked and really tender, take out of the oven, transfer the meat to a warm plate and keep it warm. Allow to stand for at least 15 minutes before carving.
4 Meanwhile, to make the gravy, spoon any excess fat out of the roasting tin, leaving a couple of teaspoons of fat behind (if any vegetables were used, leave in or remove as wished – they can be strained out of the gravy when it's made). Add 1–2 teaspoons of flour to the roasing tin and stir gently over a moderately hot heat to cook the flour, allowing it to turn golden. (If your tin isn't suitable to use on top of the cooker, simply transfer the contents to a saucepan.) Add the reduced wine, stock and redcurrant jelly and bring to the boil, stirring. Strain if necessary.

Cooking Turkey

There are umpteen different ways to prepare a turkey for roasting, but keeping the flesh moist is the main challenge. My preferred way is to cook the turkey in a closed tent of foil that's loose enough to allow steam inside. The tent is made with two long pieces of foil arranged like a very large cross. Place the roasting tin under the centre of the X and sit the turkey on top of the foil. Draw up the four sides in a box-like shape around the turkey, making a double fold at each corner to close. Close the top of the box by drawing the edges together and closing in a double fold, making a tent-like top. The tent must be loose to allow steam to circulate easily inside. There should be no need to open this tent until the end of the cooking time to allow the skin to brown. If you need reassurance and want to take a peek halfway through the cooking, the top of the tent can be opened (watch out for the hot steam) and closed as quickly as you can. After opening the foil tent to allow the final browning, pour off all the delicious juices from around the turkey, holding it carefully with oven mitts on (get help for this if you need it).

Remember to take the turkey out of the fridge at least 1 hour before putting it in the oven, which allows it to come to room temperature; otherwise it will take longer to cook. Put the stuffing in the neck end, flap the skin around and tuck underneath, holding it in position with wooden cocktail sticks. Put a lump of onion into the body cavity, along with a clove or two of garlic, half a lemon, a few sprigs of thyme and parsley and a few bay leaves for extra flavour.

NOTE: ALWAYS WASH HANDS AND EQUIPMENT THOROUGHLY AFTER HANDLING RAW POULTRY.

Approximate Cooking Times

Start roasting in a very hot oven (220°C/425°F/gas 7) for 30–60 minutes, then reduce the heat to 170°C/325°F/gas 3 for the remainder of the cooking time. Ovens vary, so these times are not exact.

The roast turkey can be removed from the oven after browning, covered with foil and a couple of clean tea towels to keep the heat in. It will sit perfectly happily like this for a good half hour before carving.

4.5–6 kg (10–13 lb):   **3½–4 hours**
6.5–8 kg (14–18 lb):   **4–4½ hours**
8.5–9 kg (19–20 lb):   **5 hours**

These times include the initial period at the higher temperature.

To check if the turkey is cooked, use a couple of kitchen paper towels and squeeze the flesh on the thighs – it should be soft. Another method is to stick a skewer into the thickest part of the flesh, holding a tablespoon close to catch the escaping juices, which will be golden if cooked and pink if underdone, in which case cook for longer.

CHAPTER 8

Chicken

If Henri IV of France could take a leap in time from the mid-1500s to the present day, he would be amazed to see how one of his wishes has come true. This benevolent monarch wished to create an economy where each of his subjects could afford the enjoyment of a chicken in the pot on a Sunday (chicken was a sign of prosperity). The dramatic success of modern intensive chicken farming has turned what used to be a luxury into an easily accessible meat, the consumption of which has been encouraged because of its low fat content.

Chicken is common to all cuisines, not just those of Europe, but also America and Asia. This isn't surprising, considering how versatile the meat is and the vast range of ingredients it blends well with. Available whole or cut up into separate joints, the choice is there to suit many dishes.

Chicken and Cream Cheese Roll-ups, page 148

Thai Green Chicken Curry

Serves 3

Thai curries include fresh herbs with their spices. Green curry paste is readily available in well-stocked supermarkets. This is a speedy recipe that also reheats successfully. The inclusion of a chopped cooking apple was unintentional at first, but the result was so delicious that now I include it regularly. The dried kaffir lime leaves are available in packets from good supermarkets, but if you can't find them, use a thin piece of lime rind.

You will need:

1–2 tablespoons groundnut oil or sunflower oil

450 g (1 lb) boned chicken (breast or leg), cut into generous-sized chunks

1 medium onion, chopped

1 large clove of garlic, crushed

1–2 thin, finger-like red chillies (see note)

½ large cooking apple, peeled and chopped

salt and freshly ground black pepper

1 x 400 ml (14 fl oz) tin coconut milk

2 tablespoons green curry paste

8 kaffir lime leaves or a strip of peel (no white pith) from a fresh lime

1–2 tablespoons basil leaves, shredded

To serve:

basmati rice, cooked according to the directions on the packet

---

NOTE: USE MORE CHILLI IF YOU LIKE YOUR FOOD VERY HOT. FRESH AND DRIED CHILLIES SHOULD BE HANDLED WITH CARE, AS IT CAN BE PAINFUL IF THE JUICES ON YOUR FINGERS GET INTO YOUR EYES OR NOSE. IDEALLY, WEAR RUBBER GLOVES WHEN HANDLING AND AFTERWARDS WASH ALL SURFACES THAT CAME INTO CONTACT WITH THE CHILLIES.

---

1 Heat the oil in a frying pan. Cook the chicken pieces in the oil until golden, then transfer to a saucepan. Fry the onions, garlic and chillies for 1–2 minutes, until soft. Add the apple and seasoning and fry for another 1–2 minutes, then add the onion and apple mixture to the chicken in the saucepan. Add the coconut milk, green curry paste and kaffir lime leaves to the chicken. Bring to the boil and simmer gently, covered, for about 15 minutes, until the chicken is cooked.

2 When serving, scatter the basil leaves on top and serve with cooked basmati rice.

Bacon and Mushroom-topped Chicken Breasts

Serves 4

A wonderful dish for a special occasion, lightly fried chicken breasts are topped with a tasty mixture of finely chopped mushrooms and rashers and then baked in cream. Delicious! The preparation of the topping can be done in advance if required.

NOTE: I USED DARK, FLAT MUSHROOMS WHEN COOKING FOR OUR PHOTO. IF PREFERRED, USE BUTTON MUSHROOMS, WHICH WILL GIVE A MORE GOLDEN, MUSHROOM-LIKE COLOUR.

You will need:

4 large skinless chicken breast fillets

2–3 tablespoons olive oil

4 heaped teaspoons finely chopped onion

I small clove of garlic, crushed

75 g (3 oz) button mushrooms or flat mushrooms (see note), chopped finely

salt and freshly ground black pepper

4 rashers, chopped finely

¹/₂ teaspoon chopped fresh thyme leaves or ¹/₄ teaspoon herbes de Provence

2–4 small sprigs of fresh thyme, left whole

250 ml (9 fl oz) cream

50 g (2 oz) freshly grated Parmesan

1   Preheat the oven to 190°C/375°F/gas 5.
2   Fry the chicken breasts in some of the oil to lightly brown on each side and transfer to an ovenproof dish, placing them side by side. Next, fry the onion and garlic for 1–2 minutes, until soft, then add the finely chopped mushrooms and fry for a few minutes more. Season with salt and pepper. Lift the onion and mushroom mixture out of the pan with a slotted spoon and set aside.
3   Fry the rashers until crispy, then add to the onion and mushroom mix. Season the mixture with some chopped thyme leaves.
4   Mix well together (or buzz in a food processor for a few seconds to chop the mixture even more finely), then spoon on top of the chicken breasts, pressing it down firmly into position. Any extra bits of topping can be scattered into dish beside the chicken to flavour the cream.

5   Season the cream with some salt and pepper and carefully pour a little over each chicken
    breast, without disturbing the topping. Pour the remainder around the chicken. Add the
    sprigs of thyme into the cream. Finally, scatter the Parmesan cheese over the lot.

6   Cover loosely with foil (butter or oil the side that touches the chicken) and cook for
    30–40 minutes, until cooked through. Remove the foil for the last 10 minutes or so of
    cooking.

7   Serve with potatoes and a mixed salad or vegetables of your choice.

Honey, Lemon and Mustard Chicken Breasts

Serves 4

You will need:

4 chicken breasts, preferably the partially boned ones

I medium lemon

2 cloves of garlic, finely chopped

2 tablespoons clear honey

I tablespoon olive oil

I heaped teaspoon wholegrain mustard

2 teaspoons fresh thyme leaves (or ¹/₂ teaspoon dried thyme)

zest and juice of I medium orange

salt and freshly ground black pepper

1 Preheat the oven to 200°C/400°F/gas 6.
2 Cut three slits across the top of each chicken breast and lay them in a shallow ovenproof dish. Cut the lemon in half, then cut one half into wedges and place them around the chicken breasts. Mix the juice of the other half of the lemon with the garlic, honey, oil, mustard and thyme. Add a little orange zest and spoon the mixture onto the chicken breasts. Season with salt and pepper.
3 Cook in the oven for 30–40 minutes, or until the chicken is cooked through. Check halfway through, and if the lemon mix seems to be drying up around the chicken, cover it with foil, trying to leave the chicken itself uncovered so that it will brown.
4 When cooked, lift out the chicken breasts. Add the orange juice to the juices in the cooking dish. If you like, thicken it just a little with 1 teaspoon of cornflour blended with a little water, then bring to the boil to thicken (it may be necessary to transfer the juices to a saucepan to bring to the boil). Taste and add salt and pepper if necessary. Spoon over the chicken breasts and serve.

Chicken Melts

'The LLR' was a frequently used expression of my geography teacher in school. Holding some unfortunate student's copybook aloft between finger and thumb, she would say in a disparaging tone, 'This is a perfect example of LLR – the line of least resistance.' There is many a time in cooking when I am all for the LLR! Well camouflaged with a little bit of this and that, these chicken breasts are definitely in the LLR category, yet they look and taste so good one could be fooled that more effort was required.

To Butterfly the Chicken Breasts

The advantages of preparing the chicken breasts this way are twofold. First, it makes the breasts look bigger, and second, it allows them to cook more quickly because they are thinner. Needless to say, you need nice chunky chicken breasts to start with, not scrawny little bits of things. If there is a small fillet attached to the back of the chicken fillet, you may like to leave it there or cut it off first, but use it too.

Using a sharp knife, slit the chicken breast in two horizontally, but keep it attached along one side, so when finished you will be able to open it out just like a book (or a butterfly). You can then use the chicken with either side facing upwards.

You will need:

2 boneless, skinless chicken breast fillets

salt and freshly ground black pepper

1–2 tablespoons olive oil

3–4 tablespoons cream

1–2 teaspoons pesto sauce

50 g (2 oz) mature white cheddar cheese, grated

**4 cherry tomatoes, cut in quarters or a handful of green or black
seedless grapes**

To serve:

a tossed salad or vegetables of your choice

1 Butterfly the chicken breasts as described above and season well with salt and pepper.
2 Heat the oil in a large, ovenproof frying pan and put the opened-out chicken breast butterflies into the hot pan. Cook for a few minutes per side, until lightly golden and just cooked. Take the pan off the heat.
3 Leave the chicken breasts on the pan, but using paper kitchen towels, soak up the excess oil off the pan (if you don't, the oil will spit and burn under the grill). If preferred, transfer the chicken breasts off the pan into a hot ovenproof dish, placing them side by

side (this is particularly handy if cooking for a number of people).

4 Pour the cream around the chicken breasts. Spread the pesto sparingly over each chicken breast. Mix the grated cheese with the cherry tomatoes and pile on top of the chicken breasts. Season everything with salt and pepper.

5 Put the frying pan or ovenproof dish under a hot grill and cook until the cheese melts a little and turns a light golden colour. Serve immediately with some tossed salad or a vegetable of your choice.

Chicken and Cream Cheese Roll-ups

See photograph, page 139

Serves 5

Cream cheese mixed with chopped herbs (or any other cheese of your choice) are used to make a tasty stuffing in these chicken breast fillets, which are then wrapped in rashers and baked in the oven.

You will need:

5 heaped teaspoons full-fat cream cheese, about 40 g (1½ oz) (see note)

5 teaspoons chopped fresh herbs (parsley, chives, a little fresh thyme, etc.)

1 small clove of garlic, finely chopped

salt and freshly ground black pepper

5 skinless chicken breast fillets, about 175 g (6 oz) each

10–15 back or streaky rashers

wooden cocktail sticks

olive oil

To serve:

tossed salad

NOTE: It's better to use a stiff, full-fat cream cheese. If the cheese is too soft, it will ooze out too quickly. A little wedge of Cambazola or Cashel blue would make for a nice change as well.

---

1 Preheat the oven to 190°C/375°F/gas 5.
2 Put the cream cheese into a bowl and add the herbs and garlic. Season with salt and pepper and mix well – the mixture should be stiff.
3 Cut a slit/pocket in each chicken breast. Season lightly with salt and pepper, then fill the pocket with the cream cheese filling.
4 Place two or three rashers, slightly overlapping each other, on a wooden board. Sit one chicken breast on top and wrap the rashers around the breast, holding them in place with a few cocktail sticks. Repeat with each chicken breast.
5 Place the roll-ups on a lightly oiled roasting or baking tin and brush the top of each one with a smidgen of oil and maybe a light scatter of some more chopped herbs. Cover loosely with a piece of foil and bake in the oven for 20 minutes, then remove the foil. Return to the oven and cook for another 10 minutes or so to crisp the rashers nicely and to cook right through. Serve hot, with any of the creamy juices that have oozed out. Accompany with a salad.

Quick Roast Chicken and Vegetables

Serves 4

For this recipe, buy partially boned chicken breasts with the skin still on (legs or thighs could also be used). To speed up the roasting time, the chopped root vegetables can be parboiled (all together in one large pot of boiling water) for 10 minutes. This dish is best eaten hot from the oven, as it's not really suitable for reheating. A point worth noting is that even though the tin will look chock full of vegetables, they will shrink somewhat in the oven.

You will need:

4 partially boned chicken breasts with the skin on

1–2 tablespoons soy sauce

2 tablespoons lemon juice

4–5 tablespoons olive oil

coarse sea salt (preferably Maldon sea salt, if you have it)

freshly ground black pepper

$1/4$ teaspoon herbes de Provence or oregano

2 large carrots, peeled and cut into short batons

2–3 parsnips, peeled and cut into short batons

900 g (2 lb) potatoes, peeled and cut into large, bite-sized chunks

1 onion, chopped

3–4 cloves of garlic, chopped

225 g (8 oz) button mushrooms

1 red pepper, seeded and chopped coarsely

1 green pepper, seeded and chopped coarsely

2 bay leaves (optional)

a few small sprigs of fresh rosemary (optional)

To serve:

gravy, either made from your favourite packet of gravy mix, adding to it the juices from the roasting tin, or make your own (see p.125)

crusty bread

You will also need one big roasting tin, enough for 4 servings

1 Preheat the oven to 210°–220°C/410°–425°F/gas 7–8 (very hot).

2 Place the chicken breasts on a wide tin (to speed up cooking, you could make three slashes in each one to allow the flavours to seep in, though this wasn't done for the photo). Dribble some of the soy sauce, lemon juice and olive oil over them, keeping the rest for the vegetables. Season with salt and pepper and herbes de Provence. Allow to stand while preparing the vegetables.

3 Put the prepared carrots, parsnips and potatoes into a saucepan of boiling salted water and cook for 10 minutes only, then drain well and put into a large bowl. Add in the prepared onions, garlic, mushrooms and peppers. Season with salt, pepper and the remaining soy sauce, lemon juice, olive oil and herbes de Provence. Toss everything together, then scatter in an even layer around the chicken breasts (leaving them still visible). Tuck the bay leaves and rosemary around the vegetables, if using. Drizzle the whole lot with more olive oil. There will seem to be lots of vegetables, but they will lose some volume during cooking.

4 Roast in the oven for 45 minutes, until everything is deliciously browned. Halfway through the cooking, turn over the chicken breasts for about 10 minutes. Continue roasting and then turn the chicken skin side up again.

5 Make the gravy (see p.125).

6 Serve the hot chicken with the vegetables, gravy and crusty bread.

Puerto Rican Chicken

Serves 3–4

Ideally, use generous-sized chicken thighs in this recipe, as they have a good flavour. Otherwise, use partially boned chicken breasts with the skin on. Serve with floury potatoes or boiled rice. This is quick to cook and reheats very successfully.

You will need:

8–10 chicken thighs or 3–4 partially boned chicken breasts

2–4 tablespoons olive oil

1 onion, chopped

2 cloves of garlic, chopped

1 red pepper, deseeded and chopped

3 back rashers, chopped

4–5 plum or other firm, ripe tomatoes, chopped

1 teaspoon tomato purée (optional)

2 rounded tablespoons chopped black or green olives

1 level tablespoon capers

425 ml ($^3/_4$ pint) chicken stock

salt and freshly ground black pepper

$^1/_4$–$^1/_2$ teaspoon dried oregano

110 g (4 oz) frozen peas (optional)

To serve:

boiled rice (allow 50 g/2 oz uncooked rice per serving) or steamed floury potatoes

1 Fry the chicken portions, a few at a time, in the olive oil. When lightly golden on both sides, transfer to a heavy saucepan and place side by side in a single layer.
2 Fry the onion and garlic for 1–2 minutes, until softened, and add to the chicken. Fry the chopped red pepper for 1–2 minutes and add to the chicken. Finally, fry the chopped rashers until they too are golden and add to the chicken. Add all the remaining ingredients except the frozen peas to the chicken. When adding the stock, you will want enough to barely cover all the ingredients without drowning them. Season well with salt and pepper.
3 Bring to the boil and cover with a lid. Simmer gently for 20 minutes, then add in the peas (if using) and cook for another 10 minutes, or until the chicken is cooked through.
4 Serve with boiled rice or steamed floury potatoes.

NOTE: If you wish to thicken the juices a little, blend 2–3 heaped teaspoons of cornflour with a little water. Stir it into the chicken mixture and bring to the boil, stirring, for 1 minute, until thickened. (Alternatively, use kneaded butter; see p.92).

NO ONE REALLY KNOWS who first discovered the uses of the olive and how to extract its delicious oil. There are indications that it was first cultivated in Syria almost 6,000 years ago. Greek and Roman literature abounds with references to the olive tree and its fruit. In the 6th century BC, Solon, the famous lawgiver and poet, introduced laws protecting the olive trees of Athens. Centuries-old murals and frescoes can be found wherever olives are grown, showing how little the methods of harvesting and pressing have changed over thousands of years. Recently, the Spanish had reason to become upset when they discovered that some of their 1,000-year-old olive trees were being sold to other countries.

In his *Oxford Companion to Food*, the late Alan Davidson describes the ripening process of the olive. At first the unripe olives are green, firm and very bitter. As they ripen, they become oilier and their colour changes from green to purple. Fully ripe, they turn black and become even more oily, but soft in texture and relatively free of bitterness.

There are many methods of curing olives for table use. There is such a variety of olives available to use nowadays – stand in a delicatessen before an array of bowls containing many of the different types and one is transported to the Mediterranean sunshine.

Chicken Casserole with Spices and Olives

Serves 5–6

This Greek-inspired casserole is flavoured with spices as well as olives. Chicken joints complete with skin and bone, which give a greater depth of flavour, are used. This reheats excellently.

You will need:

1 chicken, cut into joints (or buy enough pre-cut joints for 5–6 servings)

3–4 tablespoons olive oil

300ml ($^1/_2$ pt) chicken stock

$^1/_2$ a 400 g (14 oz) tin chopped tomatoes

1 large onion, chopped

2 cloves of garlic, chopped

1 generous glass of red wine

1 cinnamon stick or 1 level teaspoon ground cinnamon

3 whole cloves or $^1/_2$ level teaspoon ground cloves

$^1/_2$ level teaspoon ground allspice

salt and freshly ground black pepper

8 green olives, pitted

8 black olives, pitted

1 tablespoon chopped fresh parsley

1. Fry the chicken joints, a few at a time, in the hot oil until golden on the outside. Transfer to a wide, heavy saucepan or casserole. Add the chicken stock and the tinned tomatoes to the chicken joints. Add all the other ingredients, except the olives and parsley.
2. Bring to the boil. Cover the saucepan and simmer gently for 35–45 minutes, until the chicken is tender. About 10 minutes before the end, add the olives and the parsley. If you can find them, remove the whole cloves.
3. Serve with rice or potatoes and a salad or vegetable of your choice.

NOTE: IF LIKED, THE COOKING JUICES CAN BE THICKENED. LIFT OUT THE JOINTS OF CHICKEN WITH A SLOTTED SPOON. BLEND 2 GENEROUS TEASPOONS OF CORNFLOUR WITH A LITTLE WATER AND ADD TO THE JUICES IN THE POT. BRING TO THE BOIL, STIRRING, UNTIL IT THICKENS. ALTERNATIVELY, ADD SOME KNEADED BUTTER (25 G / 1 OZ EACH OF BUTTER AND FLOUR MASHED TOGETHER; SEE P.92), DROPPED IN LITTLE PIECES INTO THE BOILING JUICES, AND STIR BRISKLY UNTIL BLENDED AND THICKENED. REPLACE THE CHICKEN AND HEAT THROUGH.

Chicken and Chorizo Pie

Serves 8

The flavour of the chicken is given an exciting lift with the addition of chorizo in this dish. This meal isn't made in a hurry – it's what cookery writer Nigel Slater calls 'a belt and braces' recipe. First the chicken has to be cooked in a pot. The sauce is made from the cooking stock and the potatoes and leeks are cooked separately. The chunky potato topping is the final touch. Rooster potatoes are a good choice because they are sufficiently floury yet don't break up into mush.

Finally, everything is assembled and baked to make a tasty dish ideal for an informal party or weekend lunch.

Ideally, cook the chicken the day before and leave it to cool in the saucepan overnight. The next day, it's a doddle to strip off all the flesh from the chicken and make a tasty sauce with the strained cooking liquid.

This recipe is enough to generously fill one large lasagne dish that measures 30.5 cm × 23 cm (12 inches × 9 inches) at the top (the base of the dish measures 2.5 cm (1 inch) less each way).

You will need:
1 medium or large chicken, preferably free-range
1.75 litres (3 pints) water
1 chicken stock cube
2 cloves of garlic
1 onion, roughly sliced
1 carrot, roughly chopped
1 stick celery, chopped
$1/2$ teaspoon herbes de Provence
salt and freshly ground black pepper
175–225 g (6–8 oz) chorizo, sliced

For the potato layer:
1.1–1.4 kg (2$1/2$–3 lb) Rooster potatoes, peeled and chopped roughly into chunks a bit smaller than table tennis balls
50 g (2 oz) butter
salt and freshly ground black pepper

For the leek layer:
300 g (11 oz) leeks, washed well and sliced
3 tablespoons olive oil
75 ml (3 fl oz) water
salt and freshly ground black pepper

For the sauce:

75 g (3 oz) butter

75 g (3 oz) flour

900 ml (1½ pint) of the chicken stock

½ teaspoon Dijon mustard or 1 tablespoon fresh lemon juice

salt and freshly ground black pepper

You will also need an ovenproof dish (e.g. lasagne dish) measuring about 30.5 cm x 23 cm (12 inches x 9 inches)

1 Preheat the oven to 210°C/425°F/gas 7.

2 **To cook the chicken,** put the chicken in a saucepan (not too large). Crumble the chicken stock cube into the water. It's unlikely that the 1.75 litres (3 pints) of water will be enough to cover the chicken completely, but this doesn't matter – it ensures that the resulting cooking liquid/stock will be nicely flavoursome. Add all the remaining ingredients except for the chorizo. Bring to the boil and simmer with the lid on for about 1 hour, until just cooked. Leave to cool in the saucepan.

3 When the chicken is cool enough to handle (or the next day), remove all the flesh from the chicken and break into bite-sized chunks, discarding the skin and bones. Strain the stock and measure out about 900 ml (1½ pints); the rest can be used for soup or casseroles.

4 **To cook the potatoes,** put the prepared potatoes into a steamer to cook for 20–30 minutes, until tender. Drain the potatoes, then rinse the saucepan under the steamer they were cooked in and melt the butter in it. Toss in the drained potatoes. Season well with salt and pepper, stirring with a wooden spoon to roughen the surface. Set aside.

5 **To cook the leeks,** place them in a frying pan or wide saucepan with the oil and water. Season with salt and pepper, cover with a lid and bring to the boil. Reduce the heat right down and cook gently for 3–5 minutes, just to soften the leeks a little – don't overcook them. Take off the heat. Drain off any excess liquid and spread the leeks over the base of the lasagne dish.

6 **To make the sauce,** melt the butter in a saucepan. Add the flour and cook, stirring, over a moderately hot heat, for 1–2 minutes, without browning in any way. Take off the heat and gradually stir in some of the stock. Return the pan to the heat, stir in the remaining stock and bring to the boil, stirring all the time to thicken the sauce. Season to taste with salt and pepper and add the mustard or a squeeze of lemon juice.

7 **To assemble the dish,** spread the chicken pieces in an even layer over the leeks, scattering the chorizo evenly throughout. Don't yield to the temptation to be more generous with the chorizo, as it has quite a strong flavour.

8 Pour the sauce over everything, poking the dish here and there to help the sauce to partially sink down into the filling. Spread the buttered potato chunks evenly over the filling.

9 Bake for 45–55 minutes, until the top is golden and the sauce is bubbling through. (If the sauce has been recently made and is still hot, the dish will take less time to heat right through.) Allow to stand and settle for about 15 minutes before serving.

NOT THE LEAST of China's ancient arts is the art of cooking. In fact, from the earliest times, a sensitive knowledge of food and drink was one of the essential qualities of a Chinese gentleman. China is a very old nation, so it's not surprising to find that it's the cradle of all cooking east of India.

Freshness is everything in Chinese cuisine. Traditionally, even animals were (and still are) slaughtered just before required. One recipe I came across for fried pigeon suggests 'intoxicating the pigeon with some spirit before slaughtering. The flesh of a pigeon or a chicken, if tipsy when slaughtered, will be much more tender.' (Too true – any butcher will tell you that tense muscles equals tough meat!)

An acquaintance recently travelling in China decided on a whim to have snake soup in a native restaurant, only to discover that every course he chose after that had to include snake, because having been killed for the soup, the snake had to be eaten up and not wasted.

King Po Chicken

Serves 2

This is a popular dish in Szechuan, which is famous for its spicy food. Apparently this was a favourite meal of the governor in Szechuan during the Ch'ing dynasty, in the days of the last emperor in the early 20th century, hence the name King Po, meaning 'palace official'. Served with rice as a main dish (Western style), it will make approximately two servings.

You will need:

1 tablespoon olive oil

1–2 or even 3 finger-like red chillies, deseeded and sliced

2 cloves of garlic, finely chopped

400 g (14 oz) skinless chicken breast fillets, cut into 1 cm (1/2 inch) cubes

1–2 teaspoons chilli bean sauce (or sweet chilli sauce)

50 g (2 oz) tinned sliced bamboo shoots, drained

50 g (2 oz) tinned water chestnuts, drained

1 tablespoon Chinese rice wine or dry sherry

100 ml (3 1/2 fl oz) chicken stock or water

1 teaspoon cornflour mixed with 1 tablespoon water

50 g (2 oz) roasted salted peanuts (put in a sieve and rinse the salt off them)

2 spring onions, cut into 1 cm (1/2 inch) lengths

To serve:

cooked rice (allow 50 g/2 oz uncooked rice per serving)

1 Heat the oil in a non-stick pan or wok over a high heat. Add the chillies and garlic and cook for about 30 seconds. Lift out with a slotted spoon and set aside.
2 Fry the chicken pieces in two batches until the cubes have turned a light golden brown. Add the chilli bean sauce, bamboo shoots, water chestnuts, rice wine and the stock. Return the chillies and garlic to the pan and bring slowly to the boil. Cook for a couple of minutes to cook the chicken through.
3 Add a little of the hot juices to the cornflour paste and add the lot back into the pan. Cook, stirring, until the sauce thickens. Serve with rice, with the peanuts and spring onions sprinkled on top.

CHAPTER 9

Fish

In 1564, the year William Shakespeare was born, Queen Elizabeth I ruled over a population of only 3–5 million. (Admittedly the plague some 200 years before had taken a heavy toll on the population.) Bill Bryson, in his fascinating little book, *Shakespeare*, describes the fact that Good Queen Bess enjoyed unlimited powers to detain at her pleasure any subject who failed to honour the fine and numerous distinctions that separated one level of society from another. Laws laid down precisely who could wear what, e.g. satin gowns could only be worn by those worth over £100 a year, while silk stockings were restricted to knights and their eldest sons.

Food was similarly regulated, with restrictions placed on how many courses one might eat depending on status. A cardinal was permitted nine dishes at a meal, while those earning less than £40 a year (most people) were only allowed two courses plus soup. Despite the fact that eating meat on a Friday was no longer a hanging offence since Elizabeth's father Henry VIII's break with Rome, it could still lead to a prison sentence of three months. However, church authorities were permitted to sell exemptions to the Lenten rule and made a tidy sum doing so. It's surprising that there was such a demand, because veal, chicken and other poultry were categorised as fish at that time.

Happily, we have no such regulations controlling our enjoyment of fish dishes. What is important to us is that the health benefits we derive from eating oily fish (salmon, mackerel, tuna, etc.) are well known. The low fat content of all white fish also makes it a good choice for those on low-calorie diets, while the speed at which fish is cooked makes it an ideal choice for a busy lifestyle.

Fish is tender because the water supports its weight, thus it cooks very quickly. Land animals have to support their own weight and so require stronger muscles. It's worth noting that fish can become dry, woolly or even tough if overcooked.

The most important thing about fish is to buy it fresh. Fresh fish should never smell 'fishy'. A fresh fish smells like the sea and has a plumpness and firmness about it; it should not be floppy or falling apart. Choose a busy fishmonger or fish counter to buy your fish from, as a good turnover should ensure freshness. Ideally, cook fish on the day of purchase.

Fish can be divided loosely into four categories: white fish, oily fish, shellfish and smoked fish. In white fish (e.g. cod, haddock), the natural oil is mainly found in the liver (not sold with the fish). In oily fish, the natural oil is distributed throughout the flesh (e.g. mackerel, salmon, tuna). Fish oil contains certain fatty acids that are particularly beneficial for a healthy heart and so we are advised to include oily fish in our diet at least once a week.

The type of fish used in different recipes is often interchangeable. For example, cod and haddock are interchangeable in many recipes, while hake is a more delicate flavoured white fish. Salmon is popular because it has quite a meaty taste. Most of the salmon sold is farmed (try to choose an organically farmed salmon) and wild salmon is expensive. Mackerel is inexpensive and undervalued – it has a wonderful flavour but doesn't keep well and must be eaten fresh. Mackerel is also excellent when smoked (hot smoked and ready to eat) and can be bought in vacuum packs.

To prepare fresh fish fillets, wash quickly under running cold water and pat dry with paper kitchen towels. Remove all bones from fillets using a tweezers or small pliers (or ask your fishmonger to do this for you). Rubbing your fingertips over the surface of the fish fillet should reveal the pin-like bones.

Roulades of Sole with Cream and Prawn Sauce

Serves 4

Delicate and flavoursome, these fillets of sole (or plaice) are baked in the oven in minutes. A simple sauce of leeks, cream, wholegrain mustard and prawns completes the dish. If the sole fillets are large enough, half a fillet will do for each serving (the fillets have a natural divide down the centre). If small, use the whole fillet without dividing in two.

You will need:

2 large fillets of sole or 4 smaller fillets, skinned (see note)

4 teaspoons mayonnaise

salt and freshly ground black pepper

wooden cocktail sticks

knob of butter for the fish and leeks

175–225 g (6–8 oz) thinly sliced leeks, washed

250 ml (9 fl oz) cream

¹/₂–1 teaspoon wholegrain French mustard

24 cooked shelled prawns (frozen or in brine)

To serve:

lemon wedges

tossed green salad

1 Preheat the oven to 190°C/375°F/gas 5. Place an ovenproof dish into the oven to heat.

2 Place the fish fillets, skinned side facing upwards, on a board and spread a thin layer of mayonnaise over the surface. Season lightly with salt and pepper. Roll up each fillet, starting at the wide end so that the narrow end is on the outside of the roll. Hold in position with wooden cocktail sticks.

3 Remove the dish from the oven. Rub a little butter or oil on the base of the hot dish and sit the rolled fish in it, allowing space between them. Put a little butter on top of each fillet. Cover loosely with a piece of baking parchment or foil and cook in the oven for about 10 minutes, until cooked through (the fillets should be white all through, not opaque), removing the covering of parchment for the last 5 minutes. Check to see if the fish is done with the point of a sharp knife.

4 Meanwhile, put the prepared leeks into a saucepan with about 75 ml (3 fl oz) of water and 1 teaspoon of butter. Season with salt and pepper. Cover with a lid, bring to the boil and simmer gently for 5 minutes, until tender. Strain off the liquid and pour the cream into the leeks. Add the mustard and bring almost to the boil. Add the prawns and heat again until piping hot but without boiling. Taste and add extra seasoning if required.

5 Arrange a baked roulade of sole on each warmed dinner plate and spoon the sauce over. Serve at once with vegetables of your choice. Accompany with a tossed green salad and lemon wedges.

NOTE: To remove the skin from a fillet of fish, place the fillet, skin side down, on a chopping board, with the narrowest end (usually the tail) towards you. Hold the skin (a shake of salt may help give you a grip) and, using a sharp knife angled downwards towards the skin, start to cut between the flesh and the skin in a sideways sawing motion, until the knife begins to get between the flesh and the skin. Firmly holding the skin and working away from you, continue to cut along the length of the fish, keeping the blade angled at a tilt down towards the skin (which is quite strong and won't cut easily) until you reach the end. Discard the skin or use for stock.

Italian-style Fish

Serves 3–4

This is a handy meal in a pan. Fillets of cod (or other fish of your choice) are cooked in a pan with some vegetables and tinned tomatoes. Serve with crusty bread to mop up the tasty juices.

You will need:

2 tablespoons olive oil

I onion, chopped

I clove of garlic, chopped

175 g (6 oz) courgette, chopped

175 g (6 oz) button mushrooms, sliced

I green or red pepper, chopped

I x 400 g (14 oz) tin chopped tomatoes

salt and freshly ground black pepper

$^1/_4$–$^1/_2$ teaspoon dried oregano

pinch of nutmeg

3–4 x 175 g (6 oz) fillets of fish

I tablespoon fresh lemon juice (optional)

75 g (3 oz) grated mature cheddar cheese (optional)

1 Heat the oil in a frying pan, then fry the onion and garlic in the oil to soften them. Fry the courgette until golden. Add the mushrooms and green or red pepper and fry for a few minutes. Add the tinned tomatoes, season well with salt and pepper and add the oregano and nutmeg.

2 Bring to the boil, then take off the heat and place the fish fillets into the mix. Cover loosely and simmer gently for about 5 minutes, depending on the thickness of the fish, until it's cooked. Drizzle a little lemon juice over the fish. Scatter the cheese on top, place the pan under the grill and cook until golden brown. Serve hot.

Oriental Smoked Haddock Fish Cakes

Serves 3

Fish cakes are a versatile dish. Using mashed potatoes as a base, many different combinations of ingredients can be added.

The ever-popular fish cakes are given an Oriental twist in this recipe. It can also be made with smoked cod.

You will need:

225 g (8 oz) cooked smoked haddock fillet, skinned

450 g (1 lb) boiled potatoes, mashed

25 g (1 oz) butter

2 teaspoons olive oil

1 onion, finely chopped

2 teaspoons coriander seeds

1 teaspoon mustard seeds

1 green chilli, deseeded and chopped

1 clove of garlic, crushed

1 egg, beaten

salt and freshly ground black pepper

vegetable or olive oil plus a small knob of butter, to fry

To serve:

sprigs of fresh coriander, flat leaf parsley or dill

1   Remove any bones from the smoked haddock, flake it and mix well with the potato. Set aside.
2   Melt the butter with the oil in a small saucepan. Add the onion and cook over a low heat for 1–2 minutes, until transparent. Increase the heat and add the coriander seeds, mustard seeds and chilli. Cook for 1 minute, or until the seeds begin to pop, then add the garlic and cook for 30 seconds. Remove the pan from the heat.
3   Add the onion and spice mixture to the smoked haddock and potato. Mix together well and bind with the beaten egg. Season to taste with salt and pepper.
4   Shape the fish and potato mixture into ovals or rounds 2.5 cm (1 inch) thick and 7.5 cm (3 inches) wide. Cover and refrigerate until ready to use.
5   Heat some oil in a frying pan and add a little knob of butter. Fry the potato cakes for 3–4 minutes on each side, until nicely browned and hot. Serve hot with sprigs of coriander, parsley or dill.

Variation:

Use smoked mackerel instead of smoked haddock. The mackerel is already cooked, so simply discard the skin and bones and mix the flaked flesh into the potatoes.

Fish Cakes with Creamy Sauce

Serves 8 as a starter or 4 as a main dish

Mashed potatoes make a handy base for the fish cake mixture. Use a combination of fish for good flavour, making sure to include a smoked fish in the mix. I like to cook the fish all together in the milk, then use this milk later to make the creamy sauce.

You will need:

450 g (1 lb) floury potatoes, peeled and cut into bite-sized chunks

50 g (2 oz) butter

salt and freshly ground black pepper

250 g (9 oz) smoked haddock (or smoked cod)

250 g (9 oz) cod

250 g (9 oz) salmon

425 ml ($^3/_4$ pint) milk

2 bay leaves

1 medium–large onion, finely chopped

2 tablespoons finely chopped fresh parsley

juice of $^1/_2$ lemon

olive or vegetable oil, to fry

For the creamy sauce:

40 g (1 $^1/_2$ oz) butter

40 g (1 $^1/_2$ oz) white flour

425 ml ($^3/_4$ pint) of the milk the fish was cooked in (if some has evaporated, add a little fresh milk)

1 tablespoon finely chopped chives or parsley

juice of $^1/_2$ lemon

1   Cook the potatoes until tender. Preferably do this by steaming them, as they won't get soggy using this method. Mash the cooked potatoes with 25 g (1 oz) of the butter and season with salt and pepper.

2   Meanwhile, put the smoked fish in a bowl and cover it with boiling water. Leave for 2–4 minutes (to reduce the salt content), then drain well and transfer the smoked fish into a wide saucepan. Add the cod and salmon. Pour in the milk, add the bay leaves, plenty of freshly ground black pepper and a pinch of salt. Bring to the boil and simmer gently for a few minutes, until the fish is cooked. Lift out the fish with a slotted spoon. Remove and discard the skin and bones, flake the flesh and add it to the mashed potatoes. Strain the milk and set it aside for the sauce.

3 Sauté the onion in the remaining 25 g (1 oz) of butter for 1–2 minutes, until soft but not browned. Add the onion to the mashed potatoes along with the chopped parsley and the lemon juice and mix everything together. Taste to check the seasoning.

4 Shape the mixture into 4 large or 8 small round fish cakes. Chill the prepared fish cakes in the fridge for a little while to firm them up.

5 Heat the olive or vegetable oil and fry the fish cakes over a moderate heat for 3–5 minutes, until golden brown on each side. Continue frying gently until the fish cakes are piping hot all the way through.

6 Meanwhile, to make the creamy sauce, simply mash together the butter and flour to make a paste (called kneaded butter). Bring the strained milk to the boil and drop in small bits of the kneaded butter, whisking briskly with a wire whisk, until the sauce thickens nicely (it should be the consistency of thick cream – you may need a little more milk). Add the chopped chives or parsley and the lemon juice. Check the seasoning and serve in a gravy boat.

NOTE: IF PREFERRED, ONCE THE FISH CAKES HAVE BEEN FRIED UNTIL GOLDEN BROWN ON BOTH SIDES, THEY CAN BE BAKED UNTIL HEATED THROUGH. PLACE THEM ON A FLAT TIN IN A HOT OVEN (200°C/400°F/GAS 6) FOR ABOUT 10 MINUTES.

Three-Fish Pie

Serves 4–6

A combination of smoked cod, fresh cod and fresh salmon gives a wonderful flavour to this pie. The fish is cooked together in milk, which is then used to make the sauce. The strong flavour of the smoked fish is mellowed and adds great flavour to the blander fresh fish. There is a choice of toppings with this dish – either mashed potatoes or breadcrumbs and grated cheese.

You will need:

225 g (8 oz) fillet of smoked cod

250 g (9 oz) fillet of fresh cod

250 g (9 oz) salmon fillet

900 ml (1½ pint) full-fat milk

2 bay leaves

2 sprigs of fresh parsley

1 sprig of fresh thyme

1 sprig of fresh basil

salt and freshly ground black pepper

25 g (1 oz) butter

1 tablespoon olive oil

1 small onion, finely chopped

225 g (8 oz) leek, thinly sliced and washed

125 g (4½ oz) mushrooms

150 g (5 oz) cherry tomatoes

For the sauce:

50 g (2 oz) butter

50 g (2 oz) flour

1 tablespoon chopped fresh herbs (e.g. basil, parsley, chives)

700 ml (1¼ pints) hot milk (from cooking the fish)

salt and freshly ground black pepper

1 tablespoon lemon juice (optional)

For the potato topping:

1.2–1.4 kg (2½–3 lb) floury potatoes, peeled

25–40 g (1–1½ oz) butter

110 ml (4 fl oz) hot milk

salt and freshly ground black pepper

For the breadcrumb topping:

50 g (2 oz) fine breadcrumbs

40 g (1¹/₂ oz) butter, melted

salt and freshly ground black pepper

25–50 g (1–2 oz) grated mature white cheddar cheese

1 Preheat the oven to 200°C/400°F/gas 6.

2 If using the potato topping, put the potatoes on to cook (see below).

3 If possible, using a little pliers or tweezers, pull out the bones from the fish – running your fingertips over the surface of the fillets will reveal their whereabouts.

4 Place all the fish in a wide frying pan or saucepan. Pour in the milk, add the herbs and season with salt and pepper. Bring to the boil and reduce the heat, covering with a lid or foil, and simmer gently for 3–4 minutes, until the fish is just about cooked. Carefully lift out the fish and break into generous chunks, discarding any skin or bones. Arrange the fish in a wide ovenproof dish, distributing the different types evenly.

5 Strain the milk and, if necessary, add a little fresh milk to it to measure 700 ml (1¹/₄ pints). Set aside and rinse out the saucepan.

6 Melt the 25 g (1 oz) of butter with the oil in the rinsed-out saucepan and fry the onion and leek for 1–2 minutes, until soft. Add the mushrooms and fry for a further few minutes, until soft. Finally, add the cherry tomatoes and fry for 1–2 minutes. Season everything with a little more salt and pepper. Using a slotted spoon, lift out the vegetables and spoon over the fish.

7 **To make the sauce,** melt the 50 g (2 oz) of butter in the same saucepan, add the flour and stir to a paste, cooking over the heat for about 2 minutes to make a roux. Draw off the heat and add in all the hot milk at once. Using a whisk, stir briskly to make a smooth sauce, bringing gently to the boil to thicken. Add the chopped fresh herbs, check the seasoning, stir in the lemon juice and pour the sauce over the fish.

8 **To make the potato topping,** cut the potatoes into halves or quarters to speed up the cooking and cook in a steamer over boiling water until tender.

9 When the potatoes are tender, rinse out the saucepan and melt a lump of butter in it. Toss in the potatoes and season with salt and pepper. Leave the potatoes in chunks or mash until smooth and creamy, adding enough hot milk to give the right consistency. Season with salt and pepper.

10 **To make the breadcrumb topping,** mix the crumbs in the melted butter, season with salt and pepper and scatter the crumbs evenly over the fish filling in the ovenproof dish to create a thin layer. Scatter the grated cheese on top.

11 Bake the pie in the preheated oven until the top is turning a golden brown and the sauce is bubbling up from underneath. If the ingredients are hot going into the oven, this will only take about 30 minutes; if cold, it will take about 15 minutes longer.

Peppered Tuna Steaks

Serves 2

Just like peppered steak, peppered tuna steaks make a tasty meal. The peppercorns must be cracked first. Use a peppermill to grind the peppercorns, or if a coarser texture is preferred, crush them in a large pestle and mortar. Alternatively, you could use a rolling pin and a chopping board. However, when you place the peppercorns on the board, cover them, board and all, with clingfilm. This prevents the peppercorns jumping all over the place when you bash them with the rolling pin.

NOTE: TUNA SHOULDN'T BE OVERCOOKED OR IT WILL GO DRY.

You will need:

1–2 tablespoons whole peppercorns

2 x 175 g (6 oz) small tuna steaks

olive oil

To serve:

lemon wedges

mayonnaise (see p.78) or crème fraîche dressing (see p.188)

1 Crack the peppercorns as described above. Dip the tuna steak on both sides in the cracked peppercorns to give them an adequate covering, pressing them well into the surface.
2 Heat a thin layer of oil in a pan. When nice and hot, fry the steaks over a moderate heat for about 2–4 minutes on each side, or as liked. Serve with lemon wedges, mayonnaise or crème fraîche dressing and vegetables of your choice.

Variation:

Cut the tuna steaks into short fingers, dip in the crushed peppercorns and fry. This way, they can be cooked right through without getting too dry.

Smokies

Serves 4 as a substantial starter

Smokies are a tasty combination of smoked fish and shellfish cooked in a white wine and cream sauce, which has a nice runny quality to it and not the more usual thick and clinging variety. Topped with a little grated Gruyère cheese, each portion is individually served in a ramekin dish. Johnnie Cooke of Cooke's Restaurant gave me this recipe.

You will need:

350 g (12 oz) naturally smoked haddock, skinned and bones removed (see note)

4 jumbo scallops

8 large peeled prawns

splash of olive oil

2 baby leeks, sliced and washed well

I clove of garlic, finely sliced

100 ml (3^1/$_2$ fl oz) dry white wine

300 ml (generous ^{1}/$_2$ pint) double cream

110 g (4 oz) vine-ripened cherry tomatoes, halved

salt and freshly ground pepper, preferably using white peppercorns

90 g (3^1/$_2$ oz) aged Gruyère, grated

I lemon, cut into quarters, to serve

crusty French bread, to serve

1. You will also need 4 ramekin dishes (175 ml/6 fl oz), heated.
2. Cut the raw fish and shellfish into fairly even-sized cubes.
3. Heat a frying pan and add the oil. Fry the leeks and garlic for 2–3 minutes, until soft. Add the white wine and simmer briskly to reduce by half. (This cooks off the alcohol, which would otherwise taste bitter.) Add the cream and slowly increase the heat to a brisk simmer. Cook to reduce the sauce a little and to thicken it slightly.
4. Add the fish, shellfish and cherry tomatoes and season with white pepper. Simmer everything together for a few minutes, until the fish is just cooked. Add salt if necessary.
5. Divide the mixture between the 4 individual ramekin dishes. Sprinkle with the Gruyère cheese and brown under a hot grill.
6. Serve each portion with a lemon wedge on the side. Accompany with some crusty French bread.

NOTE: IT'S NOT EASY TO GET NATURALLY SMOKED HADDOCK OR COD, WHICH HAS A CREAMY BEIGE OR PALE TAN COLOUR THAT'S VERY DIFFERENT FROM THE EASILY

AVAILABLE SMOKED HADDOCK AND COD, WHICH ARE DYED A BRIGHT ORANGE COLOUR. ONE WAY I HAVE OF DEALING WITH THIS PROBLEM IS TO BUY GOOD THICK FILLETS OF THE BRIGHT ORANGE SMOKED HADDOCK OR COD. I PUT THEM IN A PYREX BOWL AND COVER IT WITH BOILING WATER, LEAVE TO STAND FOR ABOUT 5 MINUTES, THEN DRAIN OFF THE WATER. USING A SHARP KNIFE, I CUT A VERY THIN LAYER OFF THE TOP OF THE FILLETS, VIRTUALLY REMOVING MOST OF THE ORANGE. THE TRIMMED ORANGE BITS CAN THEN BE USED ELSEWHERE IF YOU LIKE, SUCH AS IN A SOUP.

Baked Stuffed Monkfish

Serves 3

A tasty stuffing fills the centre of this 'sandwich' of monkfish tail fillets, which are then wrapped in thin slices of Parma ham (or rashers).

You will need:

2 tablespoons olive oil

15 g ($^1/_2$ oz) butter

2–3 tablespoons finely chopped onion

1 small clove of garlic, finely chopped

4–5 anchovy fillets in oil, drained and chopped

1 teaspoon finely grated lemon zest

1 teacup breadcrumbs

1 teaspoon chopped fresh thyme leaves or $^1/_4$ teaspoon dried thyme

2 tablespoons chopped fresh parsley

salt and freshly ground black pepper

squeeze of fresh lemon juice

2 equal-sized fillets of monkfish tail, about 500–550 g/18–20 oz in total

approximately 6 slices of Parma (or Serrano) ham or back rashers

wooden cocktail sticks

275 g (10 oz) vine-ripened cherry tomatoes

To serve:

**700–900 g (1½–2 lb) new (or small) potatoes, cooked and browned on
   a pan in olive oil**

You will also need a roasting or baking tin lined with tinfoil and drizzled lightly with olive oil

---

NOTE: CHECK THAT THERE IS NO THIN MEMBRANE LEFT ON THE MONKFISH, AS THIS IS TOUGH AND CAUSES THE FISH TO CURL UP DURING COOKING. ASK YOUR FISHMONGER TO REMOVE IT. (INSTRUCTIONS FOR REMOVING THE MEMBRANE ARE THE SAME AS FOR REMOVING THE SKIN – SEE THE NOTE ON P.164.)

---

1 Preheat the oven to 200°C/400°F/gas 6.

2 Heat the olive oil and butter in a pan and fry the onion and garlic for 1–2 minutes, until they are soft but not browned. Take off the heat and add in the anchovies, lemon zest, breadcrumbs, thyme, parsley, a little salt and pepper, some lemon juice and a drop of water if necessary to moisten. Mix everything together well.

3 Lay the monkfish fillets on a board, flat side upwards, spread the stuffing on one fillet and place the other on top. Lay overlapping slices of Parma ham or rashers on top of the fish and tuck in underneath. If some of the slices of ham are too short to tuck in underneath, use two (overlapping them on top) to wrap around the stuffed fillets. Secure the ham in place with cocktail sticks.

4 Drizzle a little olive oil over the top of the prepared fish and cover loosely with a piece of foil. Bake in the oven for 15 minutes. Brush the cherry tomatoes with oil and set aside.

5 Remove the foil and place the tomatoes around the fish. Return to the oven for 15–20 minutes more, until the fish is cooked through. Remove the cocktail sticks and serve with the browned potatoes.

WITH WILD SALMON being such an elusive, expensive food, it's hard to believe that in medieval times in the north of England, apprentices stipulated that the free meals they were supplied with should not include salmon more than three times a week!

Modern fish farming ensures a constant supply of salmon in the 21st century. Its meaty flesh is suitable for many different cooking methods and recipes. It can make meals in minutes or be used for more elaborate dishes.

Two-Salmon Terrine

Serves 8 as a starter or 4–5 as a main dish

A rather special dish, this terrine (or salmon loaf) uses a combination of fresh and smoked salmon and is inspired by a recipe of Paul Rankin's. The texture is chunky, not smooth like a mousse.

It's best to chill this in the fridge overnight, then take it out and stand on the kitchen counter for about 1 hour before serving. Turn out of the tin and serve right side up if you prefer the chunky, baked appearance to be on top, as I do. Otherwise, turn out of the tin and serve upside down to reveal the smooth underside. Serve with flavoured mayonnaise (see p.78) and accompany with a few salads. Use a sharp knife to cut carefully into slices.

You will need:
300 g (11 oz) leek, finely chopped
25 g (1 oz) butter
4 tablespoons water
salt and freshly ground black or white pepper
700 g (1½ lb) salmon, all skin and bones removed, fridge cold
200 g (7 oz) smoked salmon, skinned, fridge cold
2 small eggs, fridge cold
100 ml (3½ fl oz) cream, fridge cold
1 tablespoon chopped fresh parsley
1 tablespoon chopped fresh chives

To serve:
3–4 tablespoons mayonnaise
1 tablespoon tomato relish (or lemon juice)
salad of mixed baby leaves with honey dressing (see p.89)

You will also need a loaf tin 23 cm x 13 cm (9 inches x 5 inches) or terrine dish of the same size

1 Preheat the oven to 160°C/325°F/gas 3. Line the tin with baking parchment, as this makes turning out the cooked and chilled terrine much easier.

2 Fry the leeks in the butter and water for a few minutes, seasoning them with salt and pepper. When soft, drain the leeks in a sieve and set aside while you prepare the fish.

3 Roughly chop 200 g (7 oz) of the fresh salmon and dice the remainder into 1 cm (¹/₂ inch) cubes. Cut all the smoked salmon into small cubes as well. Put the roughly chopped fresh salmon into a food processor with the eggs and cream and buzz until fairly smooth. Turn into a bowl.

4 Add the diced fresh salmon and smoked salmon to the bowl, along with the herbs and leeks. Season with salt and pepper, mix well and pour into the prepared loaf tin.

5 Cover the tin loosely with foil. Stand the tin in a roasting tin and pour in boiling water to come about a quarter of the way up the sides of the tin.

6 Cook in the oven for 40–50 minutes, until the terrine is set and the top is slightly golden (lift off the foil near the end if necessary to brown). Remove from the oven and leave in the tin on a wire tray to cool. If keeping overnight, put it in the fridge but bring to room temperature before serving.

7 When ready to serve, turn out gently onto a serving plate and cut into slices with a sharp knife. Mix the mayonnaise and tomato relish together and spoon a little on each serving. Toss the salad leaves in the dressing and serve with the terrine.

Baked Salmon with Olive-Mustard Butter

Serves 2

A delightful blend of finely chopped black olives and Dijon mustard makes a tasty topping to oven-baked salmon.

You will need:

25 g (1 oz) butter

1 shallot, finely chopped

12 black olives, pitted and finely chopped

1 tablespoon chopped fresh parsley

2 teaspoons Dijon mustard

freshly ground black pepper

olive oil

2 x 200 g (7 oz) salmon fillets

1 Preheat the oven to 200°C/400°F/gas 6. Preheat an ovenproof dish while you prepare the fish.

2 Melt the butter in a saucepan. Add the shallot and fry for 1–2 minutes, until soft. Add the chopped olives, parsley and mustard. Season with pepper.

3 Brush the hot dish with olive oil and place the salmon fillets in it, skin side down. Spread the olive and mustard mixture thickly on top of each fillet and bake uncovered in the oven for about 20 minutes (depending on how thick the fillets are), until just cooked. If liked, pour about 150 ml (5 fl oz) fresh cream into the hot dish before baking in the oven. Serve with vegetables of your choice or with a salad and crusty bread.

Variation:

Use two skinless chicken breast fillets instead of the salmon. Fry until golden, then place the fillets in the heated ovenproof dish and continue as above.

Herbed Salmon Fingers

Serves 2–3

This is a fresh, quick recipe, inspired by Nigel Slater.

You will need:

450 g (1 lb) salmon fillets, about 2.5 cm (1 inch) thick, skinned

4–6 tablespoons chopped fresh herbs (chives, parsley, tarragon and chervil)

40–50 g (1½–2 oz) butter

1 tablespoon olive oil

1 clove of garlic, squashed flat

salt and freshly ground black pepper

lemon juice

4 tablespoons crème fraîche or double cream (optional)

1 Cut the salmon fillets into pieces across their width about 4 cm (1½ inches) wide. Scatter the chopped herbs on a plate and roll the salmon pieces in them, pressing down on them to make them adhere to the fish.

2 Melt the butter in a shallow pan over a medium heat and add the olive oil and garlic. When the butter starts to foam, place the herbed fish fingers in the pan. Cook for 2–3 minutes, or until the fish becomes just opaque. Season with salt and pepper to taste.

3 Just before you scoop the fish out of the pan, squeeze a little lemon juice over it. Add the crème fraîche or cream (if using) to the fish in the pan with the lemon juice and heat through.

Salmon Filo Parcels

Serves 1

The delicate, crispy covering of filo pastry is a delightful treat with the salmon filling. There's no need to split the parcel open before serving, as we have done in the photograph (to show the delicate pink salmon inside). Thin stalks of asparagus or mangetout make a nice accompaniment to serve with this dish. This recipe serves one, but increase as required.

You will need per serving:

150–175 g (5–6 oz) skinless salmon fillets, deboned and cut into small cubes

1 level tablespoon mayonnaise

1 teaspoon fresh lemon juice

pinch of oregano

1 teaspoon chopped chives

2–3 green or black olives, chopped

salt and freshly ground black pepper

2 pieces of filo pastry (25 cm x 15 cm/10 inches x 6 inches)

a little melted butter

1 egg, beaten

1 Preheat the oven to 190°C/375°F/gas 5.

2 Put the fish in a bowl. Mix the mayonnaise and lemon juice together, add the herbs and olives and season with salt and pepper. Mix into the diced salmon.

3 Lay one piece of filo on a board and brush with melted butter. Place the second piece on top and brush again with melted butter. Pile the salmon mixture in a rectangular shape (about 15 cm x 7 cm/6 inches x 3 inches) down the centre of the pastry. Fold the filo over the filling, starting at the narrow ends. Where the filo overlaps, these flaps may be trimmed/cut off so that there won't be too many layers of pastry. Fold the other two remaining (wider) sides of the filo over the salmon filling to make a rectangular-shaped parcel.

4 Place on a lightly oiled baking tin with the folded side underneath. Brush the top with beaten egg and pierce a small hole in the top of the parcel to allow the steam to escape. Cook in the oven for about 20 minutes, until the pastry is crisp and the salmon is cooked through. Serve with asparagus or mangetout or a vegetable of your choice.

Grilled Fish Fillets

Serves 2

This simple method of cooking fish is suitable for many different types of fish (fillets of mackerel and salmon are shown in the photograph). Choose fish fillets with the skin still on to help keep the fish together.

You will need:

2 x 175 g (6 oz) chunky fish fillets of your choice

olive oil, to brush

salt and freshly ground black pepper

15 g ('/₂ oz) melted butter

I tablespoon chopped fresh herbs (parsley, chives, basil)

juice of '/₂ lemon

To serve:

crème fraîche dressing (p.188) or green tartare sauce (p.189)

1 Heat the grill to piping hot. If liked, cover your wire grill tray with a layer of foil brushed with oil.
2 Brush the fish fillets on both sides with olive oil. Place on the hot grill tray skin side up. Cook under a hot grill for 2–3 minutes (mackerel skin is delicate and cooks quickly). Turn gently (an egg lifter works well here), season lightly with salt and pepper, spread the melted butter and herbs over and grill until cooked, just another few minutes.
3 If you wish to check for doneness, use a pointed knife to separate the flakes of the fish at the thickest part (they will separate easily if cooked) and check that the colour of the fish in the centre is the same colour right through. Cook longer if required. Avoid overcooking, which will make the fish lose its delicious moistness.

NOTE: FRYING FISH FILLETS BUTTER BURNS EASILY, BUT ADDING A LITTLE OIL TO IT HELPS PREVENT THIS. I USE I TABLESPOON OF OLIVE OIL ADDED TO ABOUT 25 G (I OZ) OF BUTTER. IF PREFERRED, USE CLARIFIED BUTTER (SEE THE NOTE ON P.35), AS IT DOESN'T BURN AS EASILY. ALSO AVOID TURNING THE MORE DELICATE FISH MORE THAN IS NECESSARY AND DON'T FRY TOO MUCH FISH ON THE PAN AT ONE TIME, AS THIS WILL COOL DOWN THE TEMPERATURE OF THE PAN AND THE FISH WON'T BE CRISPY.

Seared Scallops with Noodles

Serves 4–5 as a starter or 2–3 as a light lunch

The climate of Thailand is tropical, so there is an abundance of fruits, vegetables and aromatic herbs, which is reflected in Thai cuisine. In Thailand, food is a celebration. To have to eat alone is rated high on the Thai scale of misfortunes. Cooking is a source of pride and cooks will strive for a balance of flavours. In former times, Thais were accustomed to eating with their fingers, pressing the rice into small balls, which were dipped into the dishes. Today, however, they mainly eat with spoons to scoop up the sauces, using a fork to mix and push the food onto the spoon.

The smooth texture and flavour of the scallops makes a good contrast with the spicy noodle mixture. Buy fresh scallops if you can for this recipe. Frozen (thawed) scallops will do if necessary, but they shrink somewhat during cooking.

You will need:

150–175 g (5–6 oz) egg noodles

1–2 tablespoons sunflower oil

10 fresh scallops, coral removed, slit in half through the centre to give two thinner discs

1–2 cloves of garlic, thinly sliced

$^1/_2$–1 thin red chilli, deseeded and sliced thinly lengthways (wash your hands well after deseeding to prevent any juices from getting into your eyes)

1 cm ($^1/_2$ inch) piece of root ginger, peeled and cut into thin matchsticks (or grated if preferred)

1 teaspoon soy sauce

$^1/_2$ teaspoon sesame oil (optional)

handful fresh coriander leaves, roughly chopped

salt and freshly ground black pepper

To serve:

lime wedges

1　Cook the noodles as directed on the packet. Drain and keep warm.
2　Heat half the oil in a wok or frying pan. When really hot, add a few scallops at a time and fry very quickly on each side, until lightly browned. Remove from the pan, set aside and keep warm.
3　Put the remaining sunflower oil in the pan over a medium to low heat. Add the garlic, chilli and ginger and cook gently for a few minutes, stirring. Add the soy sauce, sesame oil and the noodles. Toss everything together, adding in the coriander. Taste and season with salt and pepper if necessary.
4　Divide the noodles between 4 plates and arrange the scallops on top. Squeeze the lime juice over the dish before eating. Serve hot.

CHAPTER 10

Pasta and Rice

Young wealthy members of the elite of the 17th, 18th and 19th centuries often spent two to four years travelling around Europe in an effort to broaden their horizons and learn about language, architecture, geography and culture, an experience known as the Grand Tour. Paris and Rome were a must to visit, but a notable part of the visit to Italy was a trip to Naples to see the spaghetti hanging to dry in the streets. The hot winds blowing off Mount Vesuvius alternating with the fresh cool breezes off the sea provided the perfect drying conditions for pasta.

In Naples, pasta was a public business. The macaroni seller cooked and sold his pasta in the streets and his (not so wealthy) customers ate in the streets, using their fingers, despite the fact that the Italians were the first to use a fork at the table in Europe.

On their return home, many of these travellers wanted to show off their foreign-acquired habits – such as eating macaroni. Some had a tendency to affectation and overdressing and frequently wore the most elaborate of wigs and so were dubbed 'macaronies'. Remember Yankee Doodle, who went to town and 'stuck a feather in his cap and called it macaroni'?

Italian food changes dramatically from north to south, and the contrast in food is directly related to the local produce. Northern Italy, for example, is an area with a rich, fertile valley surrounding the River Po. Cattle abound and so butter, cream and meats are frequently used ingredients. Likewise, arborio rice is grown in the moist fields of this area. On the other hand, southern Italians are more likely to regard pizza as comfort food. With their abundance of olives and olive oil, tomatoes and fruits, they eat much less meat and dairy products. This diet, which is high in fruits and vegetables and which uses olive oil rather than animal fats, has been proved to be good for the heart.

One often associates Italy with sunshine, so it's easy to forget that winter can be very cold there, especially in the mountains. A hearty pasta dish can be wonderfully warming as the days get colder.

Basics

Used all over Italy, pasta is one of the best convenience foods to have in your kitchen press. Dried pasta requires little or no preparation before cooking. It's made from durum wheat, a hard wheat that is ground into semolina and then made into a dough that the pasta is then shaped from. The hard wheat keeps its shape when cooked. Dried pasta has an excellent shelf life, which makes it ideal for storing in the kitchen, ready for use at a moment's notice. (Nonetheless, do check the use-by date on the packet just in case.) Fresh pasta, on the other hand, for sale in the chilled cabinet, only has a short shelf life.

It's not difficult to cook pasta, but as the Italians say, 'spaghetti loves company' – in other words, don't leave the kitchen, allowing the pasta to boil away unchecked. Overcooked pasta is mushy and not nearly as nice as when it still has that slight bite, which the Italians call 'al dente'. To cook pasta, use a large pot of salted water (about 3 litres for every 500 g/1 lb 2 oz pasta, adding about 1 teaspoon salt to every litre of water). The salted water should be boiling briskly as you drop in the pasta. Stir it with a spoon to prevent it clumping together, cover with a lid and bring back to the boil. Once the water comes back to the boil, remove the lid and adjust the heat so that the water boils fast without boiling over. Stir the pasta again to prevent it sticking. There's no need to add olive oil.

Cooking time varies with the shape of the pasta. Check the time on the packaging, but start testing even before the time recommended. If the pasta is going to be served straight away, it should be tender, but the 'soul' – the innermost part – should still be firm. If the pasta is going to get a second cooking (e.g. pasticcio; see p.202), stop the cooking while the bite is still rather firm. Have a colander ready in the sink and drain the pasta as soon as it's ready (save a mugful of the cooking liquid in case the pasta is over-drained and you wish to moisten it later). Serve as required.

If serving the pasta cold in a salad, after draining, run some cold water through it to help cool it down quickly and prevent it cooking further in its own heat. Put into a wide bowl, add in 1 tablespoon of olive oil and toss to prevent it sticking together.

Pasta can also be cooked in a light stock. If liked, add one chicken or vegetable stock cube to 2–3 litres of salted water.

NOTE: FOR A MAIN DISH, ALLOW ABOUT 110 G (4 OZ) OF DRIED PASTA PER SERVING.

Egg Pasta

Makes about 425 g (15 oz)

Even in Italy, making your own pasta is a bit of a treat. If you have time, the process is very soothing. Use strong white flour (as is used for yeast bread).

You will need:

300 g (11 oz) strong white flour

salt

3 large eggs

1 Mix the flour with a sprinkle of salt. Place on a wooden board and make a well in the centre of the flour and drop in 3 eggs. Using a fork, gently mix the eggs within the well. As they thicken, the extra flour can be drawn in, a little at a time, to the mixture.

2 When enough flour has been added to make a soft dough, use your hands to mix and knead the dough, drawing in as much of the remaining flour as required to make a smooth and relatively firm dough. The kneading helps to strengthen the dough, so don't hold back! About 10 minutes of kneading is required to get a nice smooth dough that no longer sticks to the work surface.

3 Wrap the dough in clingfilm and put in the fridge for 30 minutes to rest, then take out and roll out very thinly. Cut into whatever shapes are required (e.g. rectangles for lasagne).

NOTE: FRESH PASTA COOKS VERY QUICKLY. IT CAN BE STORED, COVERED IN THE FRIDGE, FOR 2–3 DAYS.

Mediterranean Vegetable Lasagne

Serves 3–4

This recipe uses cartons of crème fraîche instead of cheese sauce for speed. Use an ovenproof dish about 23 cm × 28 cm (9 inches × 11 inches).

You will need:

9–12 sheets of ready-to-cook lasagne

1 tablespoon olive oil

2–3 x 200 g (7 fl oz) cartons crème fraîche (instead of cheese sauce)

1 teaspoon French Meaux mustard

¼ teaspoon oregano

pinch nutmeg

salt and freshly ground black pepper

Mediterranean vegetable mixture (see p.66) (ideally, this should be hot)

2 tablespoons freshly grated Parmesan cheese

2 tablespoons of grated mature Cheddar

To serve:

tossed salad and crusty bread

1 Preheat the oven to 180°C/350°F/gas 4.
2 Put very hot water into a bowl with 1 tablespoon of the oil. Slip the lasagne sheets into the water one at a time to prevent them sticking together and leave to sit for about 5–10 minutes to soften them (don't leave any longer or they will get too soft). Lift the lasagne sheets gently out of the water, allowing the water to drain off them. Set aside.
3 Empty the cartons of crème fraîche into a bowl and thin slightly with about 3 table-spoons water. Season the mixture with the mustard, oregano, nutmeg and salt and pepper.
4 Spread a small spoonful of the crème fraîche mixture over the base of the dish and arrange three drained sheets of lasagne over (to cover the base). Spread half the vegetable mixture on top. Spread one-third of the crème fraîche over and arrange a second row of lasagne sheets on top. Next spread out the remaining vegetable mixture and cover with the remaining lasagne sheets. Spread the remaining crème fraîche over the top. Scatter the grated cheese on top.
5 Bake in the oven for 35–40 minutes or until the lasagne turns a rich golden colour. Allow to stand for about 10 minutes before serving. Accompany with a tossed salad and crusty bread.

Spaghetti Carbonara

Serves 2

A handy meal in a dish. The raw egg mixture is added to the piping hot cooked pasta (after draining it) and the heat cooks the egg, which clings somewhat to the spaghetti. Rashers add the 'carbonara' to the dish, with halved cherry tomatoes and little button mushrooms to add extra flavour to the finished dish.

You will need:

- **225 g (8 oz) of spaghetti**
- **1–2 tablespoons olive oil**
- **2 tablespoons finely chopped onion (optional)**
- **I small clove of garlic, crushed or chopped**
- **4–6 back rashers, chopped**
- **110 g (4 oz) small button mushrooms, halved or quartered**
- **110–175 g (4–6 oz) cherry tomatoes, halved**
- **salt and freshly ground black pepper**
- **25 g (I oz) butter**
- **4–5 eggs, whisked lightly to mix evenly**
- **a little freshly grated Parmesan cheese**

1. Cook the spaghetti in boiling salted water until bite tender.
2. Meanwhile, heat the olive oil in a frying pan and fry the onion and garlic for 1–2 minutes, until soft. Lift out with a slotted spoon and put to one side. Next fry the rashers until golden and then lift out.
3. Using the same oil (or if you think it's a bit salty, wipe it out and use fresh oil), fry the mushrooms for a few more minutes, then add the cherry tomatoes and cook a little to soften them, seasoning with black pepper. Put the fried onion, garlic and rashers back into the pan to keep warm.
4. Drain the cooked spaghetti and melt the butter in the rinsed out saucepan. Add the spaghetti back in and heat thoroughly. Add the eggs and stir gently through the spaghetti, hoping it will cling to the strands and not to the bottom of the saucepan! Add the cooked ingredients from the pan. Stir gently and serve immediately, while the egg is still soft, sprinkled with grated Parmesan.

Fusilli with Tomato and Wine Sauce

Serves 2–3

The combination of ingredients in this sauce gives a rich flavour without much fuss. A few chopped grilled rashers add extra flavour, or use thinly sliced pepperoni or even chorizo. Some crusty bread should be served to mop up the juices.

You will need:

2–3 tablespoons olive oil

I onion, chopped

2 cloves of garlic, chopped

I glass red wine

500 g (I lb 2 oz) tomatoes, chopped

¼–½ teaspoon oregano

salt and freshly ground black pepper

I tablespoon tomato purée

175–225 ml (6–8 fl oz) chicken or beef stock

4–5 back rashers, grilled and chopped

I tablespoon chopped fresh parsley

4–6 leaves fresh basil, torn into little pieces

175–225 g (6–8 oz) fusilli

freshly grated Parmesan

To serve:

crusty bread

1 Heat the oil in a saucepan. Fry the onion and garlic in the oil for 1–2 minutes, until soft. Add the wine and simmer with the lid off to reduce the wine by about one-third. Add the chopped tomatoes and cook for 1–2 minutes. Add the oregano, seasoning, tomato purée and stock and continue simmering gently for 25–30 minutes, until the sauce is thickened and tasty. Stir in the grilled rashers and fresh herbs.
2 In the meantime, cook the pasta according to the directions on the packet. Drain well.
3 Serve the sauce spooned over the pasta and sprinkle the grated cheese on top.

NOTE: IF PREFERRED, THE SAUCE CAN BE THICKENED SLIGHTLY BY ADDING I HEAPED TEASPOON OF CORNFLOUR (BLENDED IN A LITTLE WATER) AND BRINGING TO THE BOIL.

Tony's Pasta with Chorizo

Serves 2

Tony Gavin shared one of his favourite ways of serving pasta with me and this recipe went down very well with the men in my life! Cooking the chorizo in the tomato sauce releases the spicy juices, which then mingle through the sauce, giving great flavour. Tony says he loves to use lots of garlic.

You will need:

225 g (8 oz) pasta spirals or penne

2 tablespoons olive oil

I onion, finely chopped

I–2 fat cloves of garlic, crushed

110 g (4 oz) mushrooms, sliced

salt and freshly ground black pepper

¼ teaspoon oregano

I x 400 g (14 oz) tin chopped tomatoes

110 g (4 oz) chorizo, sliced

½ small chilli, finely chopped (optional)

I teaspoon sugar

2 tablespoons torn basil leaves

Parmesan curls or grated Parmesan (see note)

1 Cook the pasta in plenty of boiling salted water until bite tender (i.e. not mushy or soft) and drain well. If using fresh pasta, you may prefer to cook it after you have cooked the sauce.

2 To make the sauce, heat the oil in a frying pan and fry the onion and garlic for 1–2 minutes, until soft, but without browning. Add the mushrooms and cook for a few more minutes, seasoning the mix with salt and pepper and the oregano. Add the chopped tomatoes, the sliced chorizo and the chilli (if using) and bring to a gentle boil, then reduce the heat right down. Season to taste with salt, pepper and sugar. Add the basil and cook everything together until nice and tasty.

3 To serve, the pasta can be put onto two plates and the sauce piled on top, or if preferred, the pasta can be added to the sauce and tossed together and then served. Sprinkle the grated fresh Parmesan or Parmesan curls on top.

NOTE: Ready-grated Parmesan cheese is easily available to buy loose or in small cartons. For the real thing, buy a lump of Parmesan cheese (often called by its Italian name, Parmigiano Reggiano). It's expensive but is well worth it!

Pasticcio

Serves 4

Italian-style meat sauces improve with long, slow cooking, giving time for the flavours to mingle and develop. If possible, make this a few hours in advance or, even better, the day before. If you are pressed for time, then use a jar of sauce. Serve this dish simply with a tossed salad and some crusty bread.

You will need:

250 g (10 oz) penne

25 g (1 oz) Parmesan cheese, finely grated

For the ragu/meat sauce:

2–4 tablespoons olive oil

1 onion, chopped

2 cloves of garlic, chopped

6 streaky or back rashers (smoked if available), chopped finely

450–500 g (1 lb–1 lb 2 oz) minced beef

salt and freshly ground black pepper

150 g (5 oz) mushrooms, chopped

2 x 400 g (14 oz) tins chopped tomatoes

1 tablespoon tomato purée

1/2–1 glass of red wine

1 beef stock cube dissolved in 300 ml (1/2 pint) hot water

1/4–1/2 teaspoon oregano

For the white sauce:

50 g (2 oz) butter

50 g (2 oz) flour

600 ml (1 pint) milk

salt and freshly ground black pepper

1 teaspoon mustard

For the breadcrumb topping:

40 g (1 1/2 oz) fresh white breadcrumbs

25 g (1 oz) butter, melted

1/4 teaspoon oregano

salt and freshly ground black pepper

pinch of nutmeg or allspice

2 tablespoons freshly grated Parmesan

You will also need an ovenproof dish measuring approximately 25 cm x 18 cm (10 inches x 7 inches)

1 Preheat the oven to 190°C/375°F/gas 5.
2 **To make the ragu,** put some of the olive oil in a frying pan and fry the onion and garlic for 1–2 minutes, until soft. Lift out with a slotted spoon and put into a heavy saucepan. Fry the rashers until golden, lift out and add to the onion. Fry the meat in two to three batches, until lightly browned, and transfer to the saucepan as well. Finally, fry the mushrooms until lightly golden, then transfer these to the saucepan along with all the remaining sauce ingredients.
3 Stir and bring to the boil. Reduce the heat right down and simmer gently for about 1 hour, until the meat is tender and the flavours have mellowed together. The sauce will thicken as it evaporates, but only cover with a lid if you think it's evaporating too quickly.

4 Meanwhile, cook the penne in boiling water until bite tender and drain well. If preparing in advance, toss the cooked penne in 1–2 teaspoonfuls of olive oil to prevent it from sticking together.

5 Just before assembling the dish, **make the white sauce** as follows. Put all the ingredients into a saucepan and, using a whisk to stir, bring to the boil over a medium heat, whisking constantly to make a smooth sauce.

6 **To make the breadcrumb topping,** simply mix all the topping ingredients together.

7 **To assemble,** spread half the penne over the bottom of the ovenproof dish and scatter generously with some of the grated Parmesan. Spoon all the hot meat sauce over the penne. Spread the remaining penne over the meat sauce and sprinkle with more grated Parmesan.

8 Pour the white sauce in an even layer all over the top. Finally, scatter the breadcrumb mixture over the top. Bake in the oven for 25–35 minutes, until golden and bubbling.

Risotto with Leeks and Mushrooms

Serves 3–4

Risotto is Italian comfort food – creamy rice with a big blob of butter melting through it. A perfect risotto should be served as soon as it's ready. Otherwise it goes on cooking in its own heat, thus absorbing all the liquid and losing its lovely, creamy quality.

A tasty stock is important for a good risotto. Stock cubes can be used, but a good home-made stock is ideal. If you roast a chicken, keep the delicious juices from the roasting tin and add them to a chicken stock cube to give it greater depth of flavour.

You will need:

1 tablespoon olive oil

50 g (2 oz) butter

1 small onion, finely chopped

1 clove of garlic, chopped

900 ml (1½ pints) chicken, vegetable or fish stock

225 g (8 oz) risotto rice (such as arborio)

salt and freshly ground black pepper

For the leek and mushrooms:

1 leek

25 g (1 oz) butter

1 tablespoon olive oil

150 g (5 oz) mushrooms

salt and freshly ground black pepper

1 tablespoon lemon juice

To serve:

25–50 g (1–2 oz) fresh Parmesan cheese, grated or pared off in curls

NOTE: USE A GLASS OF WHITE WINE AS A SUBSTITUTE FOR THE SAME AMOUNT OF STOCK, GIVING A SPECIAL FLAVOUR.

1   **To make the risotto,** melt the butter with the oil in a heavy-bottomed saucepan. Add the onion and garlic and cook gently for 2–3 minutes, until soft and a pale golden colour.

2 Meanwhile, put the stock in another saucepan and keep it at a gentle simmer (heating the stock speeds up the cooking process). Add the rice to the onion and stir to coat the grains in the butter. If using wine, add it now and allow it to cook a little. Start adding the stock about 150 ml (^{1}/$_4$ pint) at a time, gently stirring the rice until the stock is absorbed, then add the next 150 ml and so on until the rice is cooked to a nice creamy tenderness with a slight bite and the most of the stock is absorbed.

3 While the risotto is cooking, prepare the leek and mushrooms by slicing the leek thinly and discarding the dark leaves. Wash the leek thoroughly and put into a saucepan with the melted butter and olive oil. Cook gently with the lid on for 2–3 minutes, to soften. Cut the mushrooms into chunks or slices, then add to the leeks and fry gently for a few more minutes, seasoning with salt and pepper. Draw off the heat, add the lemon juice and cover to keep warm.

NOTE: IF PREFERRED, THE PREPARED RAW LEEKS AND MUSHROOMS CAN BE COOKED IN WITH THE RISOTTO, PUTTING THEM IN WITH THE CHOPPED ONION AT THE START OF THE RISOTTO RECIPE AND COOKING THEM ALONG WITH THE RICE AS AN INTEGRAL PART OF THE RISOTTO, ADDING THE LEMON JUICE AT THE END.

4 Add the leek and mushrooms to the risotto and serve as soon as possible. Scatter the Parmesan (grated or in curls) over the top.

CHAPTER II

Desserts

Everyone is entitled to a little indulgence and these desserts are just the ticket for a little personal pampering or entertaining friends. If you have any pangs of conscience about the extra calories, you can always run in the mini marathon.

The word 'dessert' comes from the Middle French word 'desservir', meaning 'to clear away', and in most European countries dessert follows the clearing away of the main course. The French tend to serve the cheese course before the dessert, whereas in Ireland and the UK it's the other way around. Interestingly enough, it appears that eating cheese has the effect of cleansing the mouth after other food, so maybe the French have it wrong. Fresh fruit makes a healthy dessert on normal days, but a special dessert gives pleasure to your guests and to family, who will always enjoy that feeling of being pampered.

Desserts can be very elaborate or very simple. Picture if you will the impressive pyramids of fruits and sweetmeats popular in France in the 18th century, then compare these to the much simpler fare, more akin to village cooking, of unfussy puddings for which the cook used their own eggs and home-grown fruit. These nourishing puddings were ideal to follow a simple meal of soup or such.

Puddings come in and out of fashion. Our modern, fast lifestyle and weight-watching concerns tend to sideline our use of these wonderful puddings. What better time to indulge than at the weekend when you have time to enjoy the delicious flavour of these homemade desserts?

Pear and Chocolate Tart

Serves 6–8

A baked pastry base is filled with a luscious chocolate and ground almond filling and halved pears are fanned out on top. The resulting moist, delicious tart has a secret layer of blackberry (or blackcurrant) jam in the base. Choose pears that are relatively firm for this recipe, since if they're too ripe they will just turn to mush.

You will need:

For the pastry base:

160 g (5¹/₂ oz) flour (not self raising)

25 g (1 oz) ground almonds

25 g (1 oz) caster sugar

100 g (3¹/₂ oz) butter

a little cold water

For the filling:

blackberry or blackcurrant jam

100 g (3¹/₂ oz) good-quality melted dark chocolate

75 g (3 oz) butter, softened

75 g (3 oz) caster sugar

75 g (3 oz) ground almonds

1 large egg, beaten

¹/₂ teaspoon almond essence

4–6 pears, depending on size

To serve:

whipped cream or crème fraîche

You will also need a sandwich tin with a removable base. My tin measures 24 cm (9¹/₂ inches) in diameter across the top and 23 cm (9 inches) across the base and is approximately 3–4 cm (1¹/₄–1¹/₂ inches) deep

1 Preheat the oven 200°C/400°F/gas 6.
2 Make the pastry by mixing together the flour, ground almonds and caster sugar, then rub in the butter until the mixture resembles breadcrumbs. (Ideally, buzz the ingredients all together for a few seconds in a food processor.) Add only just enough water to make a firm dough. Knead and put in the fridge for 30 minutes. Lightly grease the sandwich tin.
3 Roll out the pastry thinly and line the prepared tin, trimming off the excess pastry (keep trimmings in case of an unexpected hole in the pastry case). Put the prepared pastry-lined tin into the freezer for about 30 minutes or so to stiffen the pastry, which helps prevent the sides from collapsing.
4 Bake the pastry case blind by covering the base of the unbaked pastry case with a large piece of baking parchment that extends right up the sides. Pour a moderate layer of raw rice or beans (kept especially for this purpose) over the base and bake for about 15 minutes. Lift away the parchment and the rice/beans. (Should any unwanted hole appear in the pastry base, gently patch it, putty-like, with the raw pastry.) Return the pastry base to the oven for a further 3–4 minutes to dry the base, taking care not to overbake the sides. Remove from the oven and put on a wire tray to cool slightly. Reduce the oven to 180°C/350°F/gas 4. While still warm, spread a layer of blackberry jam over the pastry base.

5 **To prepare the pears,** peel the pears and cut them in half, removing the core. Slice each half pear thinly, starting at the fat end, but do not cut right through the narrow end of the pear, so that the slices can be fanned out.

6 **To make the filling,** melt the chocolate on the defrost setting in the microwave for 3–5 minutes, or until melted. (Alternatively, you can melt the chocolate in a Pyrex dish over a saucepan of simmering water, making sure the water does not touch the bowl.) While still warm, add the butter to the chocolate and stir until mixed through, then stir in the caster sugar and ground almonds. Finally, when it's cooler, add the egg and almond essence, mixing well.

7 **To assemble the tart,** spoon the filling into the pastry case, spreading it evenly over the jam, then arrange the halved pears, with slices slightly fanned out, at even intervals around the tart (narrow ends pointing towards the centre), pressing them down into the filling. (If preferred, the pears can be put directly onto the layer of jam and the filling spread on top, in which case they would be hidden.)

8 Bake the filled tart in the oven (180°C/350°F/gas 4) for 30–35 minutes, until the chocolate mixture has set and the top looks cooked. Serve warm or cold with a little whipped cream or crème fraîche.

NOTE: IF KEEPING FOR A FEW DAYS, BRUSH A LITTLE APRICOT GLAZE OVER THE EXPOSED PEARS TO PREVENT THEM FROM DRYING OUT. MAKE THE GLAZE BY DISSOLVING 1–2 TABLESPOONS OF APRICOT JAM IN 1 TABLESPOON OF WATER, THEN BOIL UNTIL THE CONSISTENCY BECOMES LIKE A THICK SYRUP.

Apple and Lemon Tart

Serves 6–8

For something a little special, this recipe, inspired by a recipe of Mary Berry's, consists of a pastry base filled with a mixture of grated cooking apples, mixed with beaten eggs, lemon juice and sugar, resulting in a delightfully moist, sharp, sweet filling. A heavy metal tin or pizza stone, preheated in the oven and placed directly under the tart tin, will help to cook the pastry underneath.

You will need:

For the pastry base:

160 g (5¹/₂ oz) flour (not self raising)

25 g (1 oz) ground almonds

25 g (1 oz) caster sugar

100 g (3¹/₂ oz) butter

a little cold water

For the filling:

4 eggs

150 g (5 oz) caster sugar

finely grated zest of 1 lemon

2 tablespoons fresh lemon juice

3–4 cooking apples (750–800 g/1³/₄ lb before peeling), ideally Bramley apples, peeled

25 g (2 oz) butter, melted

1 teaspoon vanilla essence (optional)

¹/₂ teaspoon ground coriander (optional – this gives a subtle flavour)

28 g (1 oz) flaked almonds

You will also need a round tin, 25–26 cm (9¹/₂–10 inches) in diameter and 3–4 cm (1¹/₄–1¹/₂ inches) deep (ideally with a removable base) and approximately 3–4 cm (1¹/₄–1¹/₂ inches) deep

1 Preheat the oven to 200°C/400°F/gas 6.
2 **Make the pastry** by mixing together the flour, ground almonds and caster sugar, then rub in the butter until the mixture resembles breadcrumbs. (Ideally, buzz the ingredients all together for a few seconds in a food processor.) Add only just enough water to make a firm dough. Knead and put in the fridge for 30 minutes. Lightly grease the round tin.
3 Roll out the pastry thinly and line the prepared tin, trimming off the excess pastry. There's no need to chill the pastry if putting the filling into the raw pastry case.

NOTE: IF YOU WISH TO COOK THE PASTRY CASE BEFORE PUTTING IN THE FILLING, FOLLOW THE DIRECTIONS FOR THE PEAR AND CHOCOLATE TART ON P.208 AND PUT THE PREPARED PASTRY-LINED TIN INTO THE FRIDGE OR FREEZER FOR ABOUT 15 MINUTES OR SO TO STIFFEN THE PASTRY.

---

4 **To prepare the filling,** beat together the eggs, sugar, lemon zest and juice in a large bowl. Coarsely grate the peeled apples straight into the egg mixture (this prevents the

apples going brown). Stir in the melted butter and mix well, them add the vanilla essence and ground coriander (if using).

5 Pour the apple mixture into the pastry case until it comes almost to the top of the pastry. Don't overfill, or it will simply spill out. Be sure the apple is evenly distributed. Sprinkle the flaked almonds on top.

6 Lift the prepared tart carefully into the oven (onto the heated baking tray) and bake for 20–25 minutes, then reduce the oven a little to 190°C/375°F/gas 5 and bake for another 20 minutes until set and a rich golden brown. If the top of the tart seems to be getting brown too soon, cover loosely with foil. When baked, the centre should be firm, not runny. Allow the tart to stand for a good 15 minutes before slicing. Serve with cream or crème fraîche.

Pears Poached in Red Wine and Spices

Serves 8

This is a classic French recipe for a special occasion. A full bottle of wine may seem extravagant, but you need it to give a good colour to the pears. An inexpensive deep red wine (such as a Shiraz) is the thing to use. The resulting cooking liquid is yummy. If you manage to have any left over after 'tasting', use it as a base for a fresh fruit salad (using plums, peaches, etc.) or use as the liquid when making up a blackcurrant jelly.

However, a quite satisfactory liquid for poaching the pears can be made using only 225 ml (8 fl oz) red wine and the same volume of water plus the spices. If using white wine and the colour isn't an issue, half a bottle or less is fine.

You will need:

8 almost ripe pears

¹/₂–1 bottle red wine

2 tablespoons redcurrant jelly

2 cinnamon sticks

4 whole cloves

2 bay leaves

300 ml (¹/₂ pint) water (omit if you are using a full bottle of wine)

juice and peel of 1 orange

110 g (4 oz) brown sugar

To serve:

whipped cream, lightly sweetened and flavoured with brandy or your favourite liqueur

1 Peel the pears carefully to keep their shape. Place all the other ingredients into a saucepan and heat together until the sugar is dissolved.
2 Place the pears in the liquid, laying them sideways. Cover the surface of the wine with a layer of baking parchment and then a lid (not completely on). Poach gently for 20–25 minutes, until the pears are soft but not mushy. Turn the pears a few times if necessary during cooking to ensure even colouring. Even if they are tender, they need this length of cooking time to ensure a good colour. Take off the heat and leave to cool completely.
3 To serve, cut a tiny slice off the base of each pear and stand on a pretty dish. Strain the liquid and serve some of it with the pears. Serve with whipped, lightly sweetened cream, flavoured with brandy or your favourite liqueur.

NOTE: IF LIKED, THICKEN THE LIQUID BEFORE SERVING BY BLENDING 3 HEAPED TEASPOONS OF CORNFLOUR WITH 600 ML (1 PINT) OF THE LIQUID AND BRING TO THE BOIL TO THICKEN.

Caramelised Apples on Coconut and Oat Flake Biscuits

Serves 6

This makes a pretty party dessert. The biscuits and apples can both be prepared in advance, then assembled shortly before serving.

You will need:

For the biscuits:

50 g (2 oz) desiccated coconut

75 g (3 oz) oat flakes (porridge meal)

25 g (I oz) flour

50 g (2 oz) caster sugar

65 g (2¹/₂ oz) butter

I tablespoon water

For the caramelised apples:

juice of I small lemon

4–5 firm eating apples, such as Granny Smith or Cox

75 g (3 oz) butter

75 g (3 oz) caster sugar

To serve:

I x 200 g (7 oz) carton of crème fraîche or a tub of mascarpone or 170 ml (6 fl oz) double cream, whipped and lightly sweetened

Preheat the oven to 180°C/350°F/gas 4.

1 **To make the biscuits,** put the dry ingredients into a bowl and mix together. Melt the butter, and as soon as it's melted, add the water and mix into the dry ingredients. This gives you a crumbly mixture.

2 The handiest way to shape these biscuits is to use a Swiss roll tin 25.5 cm x 18 cm (10 inches x 7 inches). Line the base with baking parchment for easy removal. Spread the mixture evenly over the tin. Flatten it and smooth the surface. Allow the dough to get cold in the fridge so the butter hardens, then cut the mixture into 6 square biscuits. Carefully lift them out with an egg lifter and place on a larger baking tin, leaving space between them.

3   Bake for 15–20 minutes, until golden. Allow the biscuits to partially cool on the tin, then lift off and finish cooling on a wire tray. Keep crisp in an airtight container.

4   **To prepare the caramelized apples,** put the lemon juice in a bowl. Peel the apples and cut them into wedges (approximately 6 wedges per apple), cutting away the core. Put into the bowl and toss in the lemon juice to prevent them from discolouring. (The lemon juice also adds flavour to the finished dish.)

5   Melt the butter in a frying pan or saucepan, add the sugar and stir until the sugar dissolves. Turn up the heat and let the mixture bubble, stirring occasionally until it turns a caramel colour. It may look somewhat curdled at this stage, but don't worry. When the colour is right, spoon in the apples (standing well back, as they splutter), adding any remaining lemon juice.

6   Cook the apples in the caramel, stirring occasionally, for 3–5 minutes or so until the apples are slightly softened, but still hold their shape. Remove the pan from the heat.

NOTE: IF YOU FEEL THE CARAMEL IS TOO RUNNY, YOU CAN THICKEN IT BEFORE SERVING BY BLENDING IN 2 ROUNDED TEASPOONS OF CORNFLOUR AND BRINGING TO THE BOIL.

---

7   **To serve,** place one biscuit on each serving plate, with a scoop of sweetened mascarpone or whipped cream on top. Spoon the apples and the caramel on top of the mascarpone or cream.

Apple Strudel

Serves 5–6

A special occasion apple tart! Traditionally made with a time-consuming noodle paste, this version is made with frozen filo pastry, which can be used to great effect.

You will need:

3 large cooking apples (weighing about 600 g/1 lb 6 oz when peeled, cored and diced)

50 g (2 oz) raisins or sultanas

50 g (2 oz) walnuts or pecans, toasted and chopped

50–75 g (2–3 oz) sugar (white or brown)

1 level tablespoon cornflour

$^1/_4$–$^1/_2$ teaspoon cinnamon

finely grated zest of 1 small orange

1 x frozen packet of filo pastry, thawed

40 g (1$^1/_2$ oz) butter, melted

To serve:

1–2 tablespoons runny honey

25 g (1 oz) flaked almonds, toasted

You will also need a large Swiss roll tin 35.5 cm x 23 cm (14 inches x 9 inches). Turn the tin upside down so that the strudel can easily slide off after baking.

Preheat the oven to 200°C/400°F/gas 6.

1 **To prepare the filling,** cut the apples into small dice to ensure they cook quickly. Put into a bowl with the raisins and nuts and add the sugar, cornflour, cinnamon and orange zest and mix well. Cover the bowl and par-cook in a microwave for 2–3 minutes.

2 The frozen filo comes in sheets measuring 49 cm x 26 cm (19 inches x 10 inches). You will need approximately 4$^1/_2$ sheets. Place two sheets of filo on a very lightly floured board, overlapping them down the length so that together they measure 49 cm long x 35.5 cm wide (19 inches x 14 inches). Brush melted butter between the layers where they overlap, then brush the whole surface with the melted butter. Place the next two sheets of filo on top, laying them the opposite way, then brush these with melted butter too. Place a third layer of filo on top. Trim off any excess and brush a final layer of butter over the top.

3 Place the filling ingredients in a long pile along the centre of the prepared filo sheets. Leave a margin of 5 cm (2 inches) at each end of the filling and a margin of about 10 cm (4 inches) on each side. Flap up the filo at each narrow end over the filling, then fold over each of the wide margins to cover the filling. Wet the edges with water to stick them

together. Gently roll over the strudel so the join is underneath and place on the upside down Swiss roll tin. Brush the top of the strudel with melted butter.

4 Bake for 10 minutes, then reduce the temperature to 190°C/375°F/gas 5 and bake for 35–40 minutes, until the apples are tender. (To test, insert a skewer through the top.)

5 Slide gently off the tin onto a serving plate. Cool a little, brush the top with honey and scatter with toasted flaked almonds. Serve with plain whipped cream or cream flavoured with 1–2 tablespoons of brandy or liqueur (e.g. Irish Mist) if you wish.

Chocolate Truffles

Makes about 18 truffles

These luxurious sweets will keep for about 2 weeks in a cool place. Bournville dark chocolate is suitable, but for something extra special, use very rich (70% cocoa solids) dark chocolate. Crushed amaretti biscuits or chopped toasted almonds make a delightfully crispy coating. I like to include some chopped toasted hazelnuts and ground almonds in the mixture, which makes it firmer as well as adding flavour and texture.

You will need:
200 g (7 oz) dark chocolate, broken into pieces
125 ml (4½ fl oz) cream
1–2 tablespoonfuls brandy or other liquor of your choice
40 g (1½ oz) toasted chopped hazelnuts
25 g (1 oz) ground almonds
15 g (½ oz) icing sugar
cocoa powder for dusting hands

Choice of coatings for truffles:
50 g (2 oz) amaretti biscuits, finely crushed
50 g (2 oz) toasted blanched almonds, finely chopped
cocoa powder
100 g (3½ oz) chocolate, melted

1 Put the chocolate and cream into a saucepan over a low heat and stir until the chocolate has melted and the mixture is smooth. Stir in the remaining ingredients. Cover the bowl and allow to cool for a number of hours until it becomes firm enough to handle.
2 Dust your hands with a little cocoa powder. Scoop out the mixture in generous teaspoonfuls and shape into balls in your hands. Place on a tray covered with baking parchment.
3 Put the crushed amaretti on one plate, the chopped almonds on another and cocoa powder on a third. Dip the rounded sweets separately into the coating of choice, then place on another tray lined with baking parchment.
4 Those to be dipped in the melted chocolate will require a skewer or wooden cocktail stick to lift them out. Leave to set on the baking parchment, sprinkling a few chopped toasted almonds on top.
5 The truffles are now ready to pack in pretty little boxes or other container.

Variations:

You might like to try other additions, such as 40 g (1½ oz) of ginger preserved in syrup, chopped, or 1 small Crunchie bar, coarsely crushed.

Blackberry Sponge

Serves 4–5

Hot from the oven, this simple dessert is hard to beat. Fresh or frozen blackberries will do nicely, or if you prefer, use frozen fruits of the forest. It's important that the fruit filling is hot when putting the sponge mixture on top, as this helps to cook the sponge underneath more quickly. Serve with cream.

You will need:

For the fruit filling:

I heaped teaspoon cornflour

juice of I orange

350 g (12 oz) frozen blackberries or fruits of the forest

25–50 g (1–2 oz) caster sugar, or to taste

For the sponge:

110 g (4 oz) butter, softened

110 g (4 oz) caster sugar

2 large eggs

a few drops of vanilla essence

110 g (4 oz) self-raising flour

To serve:

lightly sweetened whipped cream or ice cream

You will also need a wide ovenproof dish (1.2 litre/2 pint capacity)

1 Preheat the oven to 190°C/375°F/gas 5. Lightly grease the ovenproof dish and place in the oven to heat.
2 **To prepare the fruit filling,** blend the cornflour into the orange juice and put into a saucepan with the fruit. Stir over the heat until it comes to the boil and thickens slightly. Sweeten to taste with the sugar, but leave the flavour quite tart to make a nice contrast with the sponge. Keep hot.
3 **To make the sponge,** using a hand-held electric beater, beat the butter in a bowl, add the sugar and beat well. Beat in the eggs one at a time along with the vanilla essence, adding a little of the flour with each egg. Stir in the remaining flour.
4 Pour the hot fruit into the hot dish. Drop small spoonfuls of the sponge mixture in an even layer close together all over the fruit filling. It won't be possible to spread the sponge over the fruit, but don't worry, it will spread out itself during the cooking. Stand the dish on a baking tray in case any juice bubbles out at the edge.
5 Bake for 30 minutes, until baked right through. The sponge should be golden and springy to the touch, but it's very important to check that the centre is cooked – pierce the centre with a knife, and if no doughy particles cling to it, the sponge is cooked.
6 Serve hot or cold with lightly sweetened whipped cream or ice cream.

Flapjack Baked Plums

Serves 4

This recipe was inspired by one from BBC *Good Food* magazine. Plums are cooked with a crunchy oatmeal topping to make an autumnal dessert with the minimum of fuss.

You will need:

6–8 plums, depending on size

1–2 tablespoons brown or white sugar

juice of 2 oranges

50 g (2 oz) butter

2 tablespoons golden syrup

50 g (2 oz) porridge oats

a few flaked almonds

To serve:

whipped cream or mascarpone

1 Heat the oven to 190°C/375°F/gas 5.
2 Halve the plums and lift out the stone with a teaspoon. Place the plums, cut side up, in a buttered ovenproof dish. Sprinkle the sugar over the plums and pour the orange juice into the dish around them. Place a sheet of baking parchment over the plums and bake for 15–20 minutes, until the plums start to soften.
3 Meanwhile, melt the butter in a frying pan, add the golden syrup and stir. Add the porridge oats and stir until all are coated with the butter mixture to make a flapjack-style mixture. Remove the baking parchment from the plums and spoon the flapjack mixture on top of each plum. Scatter the flaked almonds on top.
4 Return to the oven, uncovered, and cook for a further 10 minutes or so, until the flapjack mixture turns a lovely golden brown. Serve with whipped cream or mascarpone.

Amaretti and Baileys Ice Cream

Makes 1 litre (1½ pints)

This is a cheat's recipe – you simply buy a block of ready-made vanilla ice cream, let it thaw just enough to mix in the crushed biscuits and a slosh of Baileys and pop it back into the freezer. Don't be surprised if the vanilla ice cream loses some of its volume when you stir it.

You will need:

1 litre (1¾ pints) store-bought vanilla ice cream

225 g (8 oz) amaretti biscuits, crushed fairly finely

about 4 tablespoons Baileys

1 Leave the ice cream out of the freezer until barely softened. Coarsely crush the biscuits in a food processor or put into a plastic bag and bash with a rolling pin.

2 When the ice cream is barely soft, put it into a bowl, add the biscuits and the Baileys and mix through. Put the bowl/container into the freezer and chill until frozen. Serve as desired.

Ice Cream Christmas Pudding

Makes approx. 1.4 litres (2½ pints)

This isn't exactly traditional, but it is very tasty. A modern twist to a traditional recipe, even adults love this. It's worth noting that the stirring reduces the volume of the ice cream somewhat.

You will need:

220–350 g (8–12 oz) jar of good-quality mincemeat

2–3 tablespoons whiskey or orange juice

2 x 1 litre (1½ pints) blocks/containers vanilla ice cream

To decorate:

Dip grapes and bay leaves into frothy beaten egg white and then into caster sugar. Allow to dry on paper towels.

1 Empty the mincemeat into a saucepan with the whiskey or orange juice. Cook gently over a moderate heat, stirring until the suet dissolves. Allow the mixture to get cold.
2 Remove the ice cream from the freezer and allow it to soften just enough to mix it. Stir in the cold mincemeat. Put it into a 1 ¾ litre (3 pint) pudding bowl and immediately put back into the freezer. Freeze for at least 3 hours.
3 To serve, take out of the freezer and put in the fridge for about 1 hour before required. If liked, serve the ice cream in ready-made brandy baskets.

IN THE EARLY 15TH CENTURY, the word 'cheesecake' meant a cooked tart made from curd cheese, with the addition of sugar, spices, eggs, etc. The basic idea still survives in the traditional Yorkshire curd cheese custard tarts. The baked cheesecake was also popular in central and eastern Europe and was brought to America by immigrants.

Yet baked cheesecake didn't do so well in the chill cabinets of the New World, and so the newer chilled cheesecake, using gelatin, evolved. Cheesecakes of either kind are always welcome as a dessert, especially in the summer.

Baked Pineapple Cheesecake

Serves 6–8

This dessert becomes more flavoursome if left to sit for a few hours, or even overnight, before serving.

You will need:

For the biscuit base:

225 g (8 oz) digestive biscuits

110 g (4 oz) butter or margarine, melted

15 g ('/2 oz) caster sugar

pinch of nutmeg

For the filling:

1 x 425 g (15 oz) tin pineapple rings, drained

2 x 225 g (8 oz) packets Philadelphia cream cheese

175 ml (6 fl oz) cream

1 dessertspoon cornflour

2 tablespoons lemon juice

75 g (3 oz) caster sugar

3 large eggs

For the strawberry topping:

1 large punnet of strawberries, chopped

juice of 1 large orange

1 rounded teaspoon cornflour

25 g (1 oz) caster sugar

1 tablespoon blackcurrant jam or redcurrant jelly

You will also need a springform tin 23 cm (9 inches) in diameter. A circle of baking parchment in the base will make it easier to lift off the cheesecake.

NOTE: A FOOD PROCESSOR IS THE HANDIEST GADGET FOR PREPARING THIS RECIPE — IF YOU DON'T HAVE ONE, USE AN ELECTRIC MIXER.

1 Preheat the oven to 180°C/350°F/gas 4.

2 **To prepare the base,** crush the biscuits very finely, either using a food processor or putting them in a plastic bag and bashing with a rolling pin. Add to the melted butter, along with the sugar and nutmeg, and mix well. Spread in an even layer over the base of the tin. Bake in the oven for 5 minutes, then take out and leave to cool on a wire tray.

3 **To prepare the filling,** first buzz the pineapple rings in a food processor until chopped very finely (or else chop by hand). Put into a bowl.

4 Put the cream cheese, cream, cornflour and lemon juice into the food processor and buzz until smooth. Add in the caster sugar and eggs and buzz again to make a smooth mixture. Mix into the chopped pineapple and pour onto the biscuit base.

5 Put the cheesecake into the preheated oven and bake for about 45–55 minutes, until the top is set and lightly golden. Leave to cool in the tin.

6 Meanwhile, **to make the strawberry topping**, put the chopped strawberries into a bowl. Heat the remaining ingredients together in a small saucepan and bring to the boil to thicken. (If you prefer, this mixture can be sieved.) Allow to cool. Add to the strawberries.

7 When the cheesecake is cold, remove from the tin and spoon the strawberry topping over the cheesecake.

Hazel Meringue Dessert

Serves 5–6

You could also sandwich these meringues with the chocolate ganache and some whipped cream.

You will need:

175–225 g (6–8 oz) hazelnuts (see note)

275 g (10 oz) caster sugar

2 tablespoons cornflour

5 egg whites

1 punnet strawberries, chopped

200 ml (7 fl oz) cream, whipped and lightly sweetened

For the chocolate ganache:

175 g (6 oz) dark chocolate

150 ml (5 fl oz) cream

To serve:

a few chopped strawberries

NOTE: Toast the hazelnuts in the oven (preheated to 180°C/350°F/gas 4) spread out in a single layer on a baking tray. Bake for about 10 minutes, shaking them once or twice, so they colour evenly. While they're still hot, put the hazelnuts into the centre of a clean tea towel and rub them all together — this will rub off most of the skins. Lift off the hazelnuts, discarding the dry skins.

---

1 Preheat the oven to 140°C/275°F/gas 1.
2 Take 2 baking tins, spread a layer of baking parchment over each tin and draw 10–12 circles 9 cm (3¹/₂ inches) in diameter, leaving some space between them. Or if you prefer to make one large dessert, simply draw 2 large circles about 25.5 cm (10 inches) in diameter. (Do not use greaseproof paper, as it will stick.)

NOTE: If you don't already use baking parchment, I highly recommend it. It's similar to greaseproof paper, except it's slightly thicker. It's a dream to peel off cakes, pavlovas and meringues after baking, whereas grease-proof paper often seems to disintegrate.

---

3 Put the nuts into a food processor with half the caster sugar. Buzz until the mixture is

quite fine, almost like ground almonds, yet don't overdo it – if you buzz them too much, it releases the oil from the nuts, which will cause the meringue to collapse. Mix the cornflour through the ground nut mix.

4   Put the egg whites into a very clean bowl (even a tiny drip of egg yolk, or any fat, will prevent the egg whites getting stiff) and whisk until the whites begin to stiffen. Start adding the remaining sugar in 2–3 batches, whisking between each addition until glossy. Add the ground hazelnut mixture and gently fold through the egg whites.

5   Divide the meringue mixture between the prepared rounds of baking parchment, spreading it out evenly. Bake in the oven for 40–50 minutes, until very lightly browned and dry to the touch. Leave in the oven for about 20 minutes with the door open and the heat off, then lift out and place the tins on a wire tray to continue cooling.

6   Meanwhile, to make the chocolate ganache, put the chocolate and cream into a saucepan and heat gently to melt the chocolate. Stir well to mix evenly and leave to cool in a bowl until it's stiff enough to spread.

7   When just cold, cut the baking parchment with scissors to separate the meringue circles, then carefully peel off the parchment. Shortly before serving, sandwich together with the chocolate ganache. Spread whipped cream over the tops and decorate with chopped strawberries.

NOTE: IF PREFERRED, THE STRAWBERRIES CAN BE CHOPPED IN ADVANCE AND MIXED WITH A LITTLE FRESHLY SQUEEZED ORANGE JUICE AND LIGHTLY SWEETENED WITH SUGAR. THEN, JUST BEFORE SERVING, SPOON THESE STRAWBERRIES AND THEIR JUICES ON TOP.

Pavlova with Fruits of the Forest

Serves 6

Named after a famous Russian ballerina from the 1930s, Anna Pavlova, because it was said to resemble her fluffy tutu, Pavlova is a wonderful dessert – crisp meringue on the outside, yet soft inside. Very few ingredients are required, just egg whites and caster sugar with a touch of cornflour and lemon juice (to give it a soft centre). You will need an electric mixer, either hand-held or a free-standing one.

A packet of frozen fruits of the forest (or blackberries) makes a delightful topping for this pavlova. The rich, deep colour of the fruit contrasts well with the white meringue and the sharp flavour of the fruit is an excellent foil to its sweetness. If available, include some black cherries (fresh or tinned). Many other fruits are also suitable, such as fresh summer berries, strawberries, raspberries, redcurrants and so on.

You will need:

For the pavlova:

3 large egg whites

175 g (6 oz) caster sugar

1 rounded teaspoon cornflour

1 teaspoon lemon juice

about 175 ml (6 fl oz) whipped cream, lightly sweetened

For the fruits of the forest sauce:

juice of 1 large orange

350 g (12 oz) frozen fruits of the forest or summer fruits (see note on p.233)

50–75 g (2–3 oz) caster sugar

1 heaped teaspoon cornflour

NOTE: OVENS CAN VARY A LOT AT LOW TEMPERATURES, SO ADJUST YOURS IF NECESSARY. THE COLOUR OF THE PAVLOVA SHOULD BE FAIRLY WHITE OR A PALE GOLD WHEN COOKED AND IT SHOULD BE WELL DRIED ON THE OUTSIDE. IT WILL TAKE AN HOUR TO COOK, SO CHECK AFTER ABOUT 20 MINUTES AND LOWER OR RAISE THE TEMPERATURE IF REQUIRED.

---

1 Preheat the oven to 150°C/300°F/gas 2.
2 To prepare the baking tin, place a sheet of baking parchment on a wide baking tin and draw a circle 20.5–23 cm (8–9 inches) in diameter. Do not trim the paper – leave it much large than the circle, as this makes it easier to peel off after cooking. (Do not use greaseproof paper, as it will stick; see note on p.229.)

3 Put the egg whites into a very clean bowl (even a tiny drip of egg yolk, or any fat, will prevent the egg whites getting stiff) and whisk until the whites begin to stiffen. Then gradually add the sugar, about a tablespoonful at a time, whisking between each addition. When almost all the sugar has been added, whisk in the cornflour and lemon juice with the last of the sugar.

4 The meringue mixture should be very stiff – it shouldn't move even if the bowl is turned upside down. Spoon the mixture onto the baking parchment and shape into the marked circle. Shape the sides of the pavlova just a little higher than the centre, a bit like a saucer.

5 Bake in the oven for 1 hour. Turn off the oven, open the door and leave the cooked pavlova in the oven for about 30 minutes or so to cool.

6 While the pavlova is cooking, prepare the topping. Put the orange juice and frozen berries into a saucepan. Cook gently to thaw, then add the sugar and stir to dissolve. Blend the cornflour with a dribble of water and some of the hot liquid from the saucepan. Mix well, then stir the cornflour mixture into the berries in the saucepan. Bring to the boil, stirring to thicken. If a thicker consistency is required, more cornflour can be added (in the same way). Taste for sweetness, but remember that the meringue is very sweet. Allow to get completely cold before using on the pavlova.

7 When the pavlova is cold, carefully peel off the paper from the base of the pavlova and place on a serving plate. Just before serving, spread a layer of the whipped cream over the top and spoon the fruit on top. Accompany with extra whipped cream if liked.

NOTE: If preferred, use half the above topping and add 110 G (4 OZ) fresh strawberries and 175 G (6 OZ) fresh (or tinned) black cherries.

CHAPTER 12

Breads and Baking

I can still remember my keen sense of disappointment, standing at my mother's side, hardly tall enough to reach the countertop, when I discovered that she had bought a rubber spatula to scrape out the cake mixture from the bowl. This gadget more or less shattered my little treat of licking out the bowl after she made the cake, as it left almost nothing behind!

Many of the new foods brought to Europe from Latin America by the Spanish explorers, such as the tomato, red and green peppers and the potato, could be grown in Europe. However, the tropical cacao tree could not. Spain held most of the lands where the cacao tree grew at that time, with Portugal owning the remaining areas. For well over 100 years after the discovery of drinking chocolate (made from the beans of the cacao tree), its production and consumption remained a monopoly jealously guarded by the Spanish. Despite being rather slow at the start to accept this somewhat bitter drink, the Spanish then living in Mexico grew so fond of it that they 'would die for their chocolate'.

The English Dominican priest Thomas Gage wrote in 1648 that in the city of Chiapa Real, the women insisted their maids bring them cups of drinking chocolate during Mass. The bishop disapproved of the disruption and proclaimed that anyone who ate or drank in church would be excommunicated. After some fisticuffs and a bit of swordplay, the women, who would not be denied their drink of chocolate, stayed away from Mass, until one day the bishop suddenly took ill and died. Rumour had it that he had drunk a poisoned cup of chocolate!

Cheese Scones, page 255

Crunchy Chocolate Bakewell Tart

Serves 8

This is one of my favourite tarts, which is suitable as a dessert. It is wonderfully rich and moist and keeps for at least 2 weeks. Instead of the more traditional pastry case base, I prefer to use a crushed biscuits and melted butter base (just like a cheesecake base). For a real touch of luxury, serve the slices with a fruits of the forest sauce and some whipped cream.

You will need:

For the crushed biscuit base:

225 g (8 oz) digestive biscuits, crushed

110 g (4 oz) butter, melted

For the filling:

4–5 tablespoons blackcurrant jam, softened with a spoon

175 g (6 oz) butter

175 g (6 oz) caster sugar

3 large eggs

$\frac{1}{2}$ teaspoon almond essence

100 g (3$\frac{1}{2}$ oz) chopped blanched almonds

100 g (3$\frac{1}{2}$ oz) ground almonds

150 g (5 oz) dark chocolate, melted and partly cooled

small handful of flaked almonds

To serve:

fruits of the forest sauce (see p.232) or 375 g (12 oz) mixed fresh
    summer berries

about 175 ml (6 fl oz) whipped cream, lightly sweetened

You will also need a springform tin 23 cm (9 inches) in diameter

---

NOTE: IT'S WORTH NOTING THAT IF THE TIN SIZES RECOMMENDED AREN'T ADHERED TO, CAKES MAY BE THICKER (IF SMALLER) OR THINNER (IF LARGER), WHICH CAN AFFECT THE COOKING TIMES.

---

1 Preheat the oven to 190°C/375°F/gas 5.

2 **To make the biscuit base**, mix the crushed biscuits and melted butter together and

spread in an even layer over the base of the tin, pressing the mixture down firmly.

3 Bake in the oven for about 5 minutes, just to lightly crisp the biscuits. There will be no change in appearance. Stand the tin on a wire tray to cool while you prepare the filling.

4 Reduce the oven to 180°C/350°F/gas 4.

5 **To make the filling,** spread the jam carefully in a thin layer over the cooled biscuit base, leaving a 2.5 cm (1 inch) margin all the way around. This is to ensure that the jam doesn't ooze out at the edges and get too highly baked on the sides, spoiling the appearance of the finished cake.

6 Beat the butter and caster sugar together in a bowl until soft. Add in the eggs, one at a time, and almond essence and beat well. Mix together the chopped almonds and the ground almonds and stir into the butter/sugar mixture, then stir the melted chocolate through. Pour into the tin over the biscuit base and scatter the flaked almonds over the surface.

7 Bake for about 40 minutes – reduce the temperature a little halfway through if the tart is cooking too quickly. It's ready when the almond mixture has become set on the outside but the filling is still slightly wobbly in the centre. Stand the tin on a wire tray for about 15 minutes to allow it to cool. With a sharp knife, loosen the edges, then release the spring clip sides of the tin and leave the tart to cool completely.

8 To serve, carefully slide off the base of the tin onto a serving plate. Serve with fruits of the forest sauce and some whipped cream.

Dark Chocolate Cake

Serves 8–10

Dark and sultry, a chocolate cake recipe is a must in every cook's repertoire, and this is one of my favourites.

It took me a long time to evolve this recipe to my liking, with its lovely dark sponge that cuts well. It will keep for at least 2–3 weeks, covered by a dome or upturned bowl in a cool place.

Serve in thin slices, as this is rich. Use a good-quality chocolate with a high percentage of cocoa solids (check the label). I frequently use Cadbury's dark Bournville chocolate.

You will need:

200 g (7 oz) butter (unsalted if preferred), plus extra for greasing

200 g (7 oz) good-quality dark chocolate

1½ tablespoons dark rum

160 g (5½ oz) self-raising flour

50 g (2 oz) ground almonds

20 g (¾ oz) cocoa powder, sieved if necessary to remove any lumps

4 large or 5 medium eggs, separated

150 g (5 oz) caster sugar

For the filling:

3–4 tablespoons blackcurrant or apricot jam

50 g (2 oz) toasted chopped hazelnuts (optional)

chocolate ganache icing (see p.240)

You will also need a 23 cm (9 inch) springform tin

1 Preheat the oven to 180°C/350°F/gas 4. Grease the tin with butter and line the base and sides with baking parchment, which will stick to the butter.

2 Put the butter, chocolate and rum into a Pyrex bowl and place over a saucepan of gently simmering water (making sure the base of the bowl doesn't touch the water), until melted. Alternatively, put these ingredients in the microwave on the defrost setting for about 6 minutes, or until melted. Stir the melted ingredients together thoroughly and leave on the counter to cool.

3 In a separate bowl, mix together the flour, ground almonds and cocoa powder and set aside.

4 In another bowl, beat the egg yolks with 150 g (5 oz) of the caster sugar until nice and creamy. Add the cooled chocolate mixture to the egg yolks and mix well together, then stir in the flour and ground almond mixture.

5   In a clean bowl, whisk the egg whites with the remaining 25 g (1 oz) of caster sugar until fairly stiff, but not quite as stiff as when making meringues. Briskly stir one-third of the egg whites through the egg/chocolate mixture, then add the remainder in two batches, stirring gently but firmly to mix thoroughly. The volume of the egg whites will collapse quite considerably as you mix them through the chocolate mixture.

6   Pour the cake mix into the prepared tin, spreading it out evenly. Bake for about 40 minutes, until the top is firm and the inside is set (test with a skewer pierced gently into the centre). If any chocolate dough sticks to the skewer, continue cooking a little longer. Stand the tin on a wire tray to cool a little, then remove the sides of the tin and leave on the base to cool completely.

7   When cold, lift the cake off the base and peel off the parchment. Slit the cake horizontally in two with a large knife. Mix the jam and hazelnuts together, then spread the jam mixture liberally over the cut surface of the lower half and replace the top half. Put on a serving plate and cover the top and sides with the chocolate ganache icing. Serve in small slices.

NOTE: MAKE A RING-SHAPED CHOCOLATE CAKE USING THE ABOVE RECIPE. USE AN EMPTY CAN (E.G. A 425 G/14 OZ CAN OF PEAS) AND LINE THE OUTSIDE NEATLY WITH BAKING PARCHMENT OR FOIL. PUT A RAW POTATO INSIDE THE TIN FOR WEIGHT. STAND THIS IN THE EXACT CENTRE OF THE LINED SPRINGFORM TIN AND SPOON THE CAKE MIXTURE EVENLY AROUND IT. BAKE AS DIRECTED. LEAVE TO COOL IN THE TIN ON A WIRE TRAY. FILL AND ICE THE CAKE AS DESCRIBED ABOVE. A LOVELY CAKE TO SLICE.

Chocolate Ganache Icing

Makes about 400 ml (³/₄ pint)

Ganache is a French term for a smooth mixture of chocolate and cream. It's very runny when it's hot, but it sets as it cools (just like butter), so wait for it to set firmly enough to spread easily. If you get impatient and use it too soon, it will run down the sides of the cake. Use half the quantities below to cover only the top of the cake.

You will need:

250 ml (9 fl oz) cream

300 g (10¹/₂ oz) good-quality dark chocolate, broken into squares or small pieces

1   Heat the cream in a saucepan until little bubbles appear around the edges. Take off the heat and add the chocolate, stirring until it has melted. If necessary, heat the mixture a little more. Transfer to a bowl and allow it to cool until stiff enough to pour or spread.

Amaretti and Chocolate Cake

Serves 6

I have adapted this rich but simple chocolate cake from an American recipe. The finished cake is very thin and has a textured look because of the coarsely chopped amaretti biscuits and almonds in the mixture. (Amaretti are Italian macaroon biscuits with a distinctive almond flavour.) When cut, the thin slices should be moist inside with a rich chocolate flavour. Better-quality chocolate means a better flavour. Serve it with a little whipped cream flavoured with a hint of brandy. Alternatively, serve a little scoop of ice cream or a spoonful of soured cream with each slice.

You will need:

110 g (4 oz) good-quality dark chocolate

110 g (4 oz) amaretti biscuits

50 g (2 oz) blanched almonds, toasted and chopped

110 g (4 oz) unsalted butter, at room temperature

110 g (4 oz) caster sugar

3 large eggs, at room temperature

1 teaspoon cocoa powder

1 teaspoon icing sugar

You will also need a round sandwich tin 20.5 (8 inches) in diameter, preferably with a removable base

---

NOTE: THIS CAKE IS EVEN BETTER IF MADE THE DAY BEFORE YOU PLAN TO SERVE IT.

---

1 Preheat the oven to 180°C/350°F/gas 4.
2 Lightly grease the sandwich tin with butter and dust lightly with flour, then put a circle of baking parchment in the base to make it easier to turn out the cake later on.
3 Melt the chocolate either in a bowl over a pot of gently simmering water, taking care that the water doesn't touch the bottom of the bowl, or on the defrost setting of your microwave for about 5 minutes or so.
4 Put the amaretti into a food processor and buzz for a few seconds, until they're coarsely chopped. If you don't have a processor, try putting the biscuits in a plastic bag and bashing them with a rolling pin. Mix the chopped almonds and amaretti together and set aside.
5 Next, using an electric hand-held mixer, put the butter into a bowl and beat in the sugar until soft, then beat in the eggs. Add the amaretti and almond mixture, then stir in the melted chocolate (while still moderately warm) until it's evenly mixed. (The warmth of the chocolate will prevent the mixture looking curdled.)
6 Pour the chocolate amaretti mixture into the prepared tin and spread evenly. Bake for about 25 minutes, until the cake sets on top (it will be quite brittle) and seems moist yet set underneath. Stand the tin on a wire tray to cool completely, then carefully invert onto a plate. Turn right side up onto a serving plate and dust lightly with the cocoa and icing sugar.

Chocolate Cake Fruit Basket

Serves 6

The chocolate cake is made from eggs and melted chocolate – nothing else. You might be puzzled by the way the cake rises up in the oven and subsequently sinks right down in the middle when cooled, but this is what results in the basket/bowl shape. The edges will appear rather broken looking, but don't worry, because it will be filled right up with whipped cream and topped with fruit. Use a good-quality chocolate (Bournville dark chocolate is suitable).

You will need:

200 g (7 oz) dark chocolate

5 large eggs, separated

150 g (5 oz) caster sugar

$\frac{1}{2}$ teaspoon vanilla essence

To serve:

350 g (12 oz) summer berries (strawberries, raspberries, etc.)

a little caster sugar

2–3 tablespoons blackberry or blackcurrant jam, softened by stirring

175 ml (6 fl oz) whipped cream, lightly sweetened

You will also need a 23 cm (9 inch) springform tin

1 Preheat the oven to 190°C/375°F/gas 5. Line the base of the springform tin with baking parchment and lightly grease the sides.

2 Melt the chocolate either in a bowl over a pot of gently simmering water, taking care that the water doesn't touch the bottom of the bowl, or on the defrost setting of your microwave for about 6 minutes or so. When melted, stir well and allow to cool slightly.

3 Put the egg yolks into a separate bowl with 75 g (3 oz) of the caster sugar and the vanilla essence and beat until creamy.

4 In another very clean bowl, whisk the egg whites with the remaining caster sugar until stiff, though not quite as stiff as when making meringues.

5 Mix the cooled chocolate mixture into the egg yolk mixture and beat together. Add one-third of the beaten egg whites to the mixture and whisk through, then add the remaining egg whites, folding and stirring gently until thoroughly mixed through.

6 Turn into the prepared tin and spread out evenly. Bake for 20–25 minutes, until the top is well risen and crisp. The sponge will be set but not very firm. Take the cake out of the oven and stand the tin on a wire tray. As it cools, the top will collapse down in the middle but the edges will stay standing. Gently unclip the sides of the tin, taking care not to break the fragile cake edges. Leave to cool completely (still standing on the base of the tin). When completely cold, lift off the base of the tin and remove the parchment if it's convenient.

7 If the strawberries are very large, chop them, mix with the other berries and dust with caster sugar.

8 To serve, place the cake on a serving plate. Spread the jam gently into the bowl–like top of the cake, but not on the edges. Spread the whipped cream over the jam, then spoon the prepared fruit mixture on top. Allow to stand for 1 hour or so before serving.

Summer Sponge Cake

Serves 4-6

Light as a feather, an egg sponge is real summer food. The texture depends on the amount of tiny air bubbles that are trapped in the mixture. These will expand in the oven. No raising agent is required.

You will need:

For the sponge:

4 large eggs at room temperature (not cold from the fridge)

110 g (4 oz) caster sugar

½ teaspoon vanilla essence

110 g (4 oz) flour (not self-raising)

For the filling:

poached blueberries (see p. 251)

1–2 tablespoons blackcurrant jam (optional)

200 ml (7 fl oz) cream, whipped and lightly sweetened

strawberries and blueberries, for decoration

You will also need 2 sandwich tins 18 cm (7 inches) in diameter

1 Preheat the oven to 190°C/375°F/gas 5.
2 Using an electric mixer, whisk the eggs with the caster sugar and vanilla essence until pale and doubled in volume. This can take some time, depending on the temperature of the kitchen, etc. You can judge when it is whisked enough by lifting up the beaters and making a figure of eight with the trail of mixture that falls back onto the surface of the sponge. This should hold its shape on the surface for 1 minute before sinking back down. Stop beating then: if you over-beat the mixture it will go flat.
3 Sift the flour and, using a metal spoon, gently stir and 'cut' the flour through the mixture, preserving the bubbles and ensuring that no pockets of flour are left.
4 Divide between the two tins and gently spread out. Bake for about 15–18 minutes or until golden and the edge of the sponge begins to draw away slightly from the tin. When it is cooked, the surface will spring back when pressed lightly.
5 Turn out and allow to cool on a wire tray.
6 Sandwich together with half the poached blueberries (allowing the juices to go into the sponge), the jam and half the cream. Spread the remaining half of the poached blueberries on the top. Cover with the whipped cream and decorate with the strawberries and blueberries. Leave for an hour before slicing.

Mincemeat and Almond Shortbread

Serves 8

A real treat, this recipe has become a seasonal must at Christmas in our house. It also makes a lovely gift.

You will need:
225 g (8 oz) butter or margarine, softened
110 g (4 oz) caster sugar
¼ teaspoon almond essence
225 g (8 oz) flour
110 g (4 oz) finely chopped blanched almonds
200 g (7 oz) mincemeat
1 tablespoon brandy or whiskey
25–50 g (1–2 oz) chopped or flaked almonds, to decorate

You will also need a springform tin 23 cm (9 inches) in diameter

1 Preheat the oven to 170°C/325°F/gas 3 and grease the springform tin.
2 To make the shortbread, beat the butter until soft, then beat in the caster sugar and almond essence until soft and creamy.
3 In a separate bowl, mix together the flour and almonds and beat into the butter/sugar mixture to form a dough. Use your hands to gather the dough into a lump. (If the dough is a bit too soft, put it into the fridge to stiffen for about 15 minutes.) Divide the dough in two.
4 **To make the bottom layer,** roll out one half of the dough into a small circle. Place it in the base of the tin and press it down with your knuckles or roll with a small jar (e.g. a mustard jar) to cover the base of the tin. Make sure there are no holes in the dough.
5 **To make the filling,** mix the brandy into the mincemeat and spread in a layer over the shortbread, leaving a 2.5 cm (1 inch) margin all around the edge. Moisten the margin with water.
6 **To make the top layer,** roll out the remaining dough on a round bread board dusted with flour to almost the same size as the tin, then gently slide the circle of shortbread off the board and on top of the mincemeat. Do this carefully, because once in place it isn't easy to shift it around. Press the edges together with a fork to seal, and scatter the chopped almonds over the top. Pierce the top layer (only) with a fork in a number of places to allow the steam from the mincemeat to escape.
7 Bake in the oven for 45–50 minutes, until the top is a pale golden colour and everything is cooked through. Remove from the oven and stand the tin on a wire tray. While it's still cooling, loosen the edges with a sharp knife and remove the side of the tin. Allow to cool completely, then cut into thin wedges with a sharp knife.

Chocolate Nut Cookies

Makes about 16–20

An easy American recipe, these crunchy cookies are seriously nice. When cold, store them in airtight plastic bags.

You will need:

175 g (6 oz) hazelnuts

110 g (4 oz) butter or margarine, at room temperature

175 g (6 oz) light brown sugar

4 teaspoons finely grated orange zest

$1/2$ teaspoon vanilla essence

1 large egg

150 g (5 oz) self-raising flour

75 g (3 oz) dark chocolate, chopped small

1–2 tablespoons orange juice

1   Preheat the oven to 190°C/375°F/gas 5. Line 2 baking tins with baking parchment.
2   Spread the nuts on a baking sheet and cook in the preheated oven for about 5 minutes, shaking them once or twice so that they colour evenly. While they're still hot, put the hazelnuts into the centre of a clean tea towel and rub them all together – this will rub off most of the skins. Lift off the hazelnuts, discarding the dry skins. Chop the nuts, ensuring they're neither too fine nor too coarse (see note).

NOTE: IT'S HARD TO CHOP HAZELNUTS, AS THEY TEND TO ROLL AROUND. I FIND THE HANDIEST WAY TO CHOP THEM IS TO PUT THEM ON A CHOPPING BOARD, COVER THEM WITH A TEA TOWEL AND BASH THEM WITH A ROLLING PIN.

3   Using a hand-held electric mixer, beat the butter, brown sugar, orange zest and vanilla essence until soft. Beat in the egg. Stir in the flour, then mix in the chopped chocolate and the nuts. The mixture will be very stiff. Mix in the orange juice to soften it just a little.

NOTE: SINCE THESE COOK SO QUICKLY, YOU MIGHT FIND IT HANDY TO BAKE A FEW FIRST AND JUDGE FOR YOURSELF WHAT SIZE YOU'D LIKE TO MAKE THEM.

4   Place the mixture in dessertspoonfuls on the lined baking tins, spacing them about 5 cm (2 inches) apart. Bake the cookies for 13–15 minutes, until they're nicely browned. Using an egg lifter, carefully lift onto a wire tray to cool. These cookies are soft when they come out of the oven but stiffen quickly to a delicious crispness when cooled.
5   Store in an airtight container, or put in small batches in airtight bags.

Rice Krispie and Oatmeal Squares

Makes about 20 squares

This recipe is an idea I got from a magazine yonks ago. The addition of the Rice Krispies to the oatmeal mixture gives a light crunchiness to the normally dense oatmeal mixture. These are so easy to make.

You will need:

150 g (5 oz) butter or margarine

75 g (3 oz) sugar (brown or white)

75 g (3 oz) honey or golden syrup

250 g (9 oz) porridge oats

75 g (3 oz) raisins or sultanas (optional)

50 g (2 oz) Rice Krispies

1 Preheat the oven to 190°C/375°F/gas 5. Grease a baking tray 23 cm x 33 cm (9 inches x 13 inches).

2 Put the butter in a saucepan. Add the sugar and honey (or syrup) and melt together over a low heat, stirring occasionally. Remove from the heat and cool a little.

3 In a separate bowl, mix together the oats, raisins (if using) and Rice Krispies. Add this mixture to the melted ingredients, stirring well. Spread the mixture in the prepared tin and bake for about 15 minutes, until pale golden brown. Cool in the tin or a wire tray. When cold, cut into squares.

Poached Blueberries

Makes about 175 ml (6 fl oz)

Turn a simple packet of fresh blueberries into a tasty sauce. It shouldn't be too sweet in order to provide a lovely contrast. Use as a filling for the Summer Sponge Cake (see p. 244) or simply serve with ice cream.

You will need:

150 ml (5 fl oz) fresh orange juice

1 rounded teaspoon cornflour

125 g (4¹/₂ oz) blueberries

1 tablespoon blackcurrant jam

1–2 teaspoons caster sugar

1   Blend the orange juice into the cornflour in a small saucepan. Add the blueberries and the jam to the saucepan. Bring quickly to the boil, stirring all the time to thicken the juices slightly. Draw off the heat, sweeten with the caster sugar and cover with a lid (to prevent evaporation) and leave to get cold. Serve hot or cold, as required.

NOTE: IF LEFT TO STAND FOR A FEW HOURS THE COLOUR OF THE SAUCE BECOMES MORE PURPLE — LIKE THE BLUEBERRIES.

NOTE: ADD A DASH OF BLACKCURRANT LIQUER (CRÈME DE CASSIS) IF LIKED

Raspberry and Almond Tray Bake

Makes 12

The sharp flavour of the raspberries is delightful with the almond shortbread-like mixture. You can use fresh or frozen raspberries, though I find it handy to use the frozen ones. Allow them to thaw before using, but don't allow them to get too soggy and wet. If using from frozen, the cooking time will be longer.

You will need:

250g (9 oz) self-raising flour

50g (2 oz) ground almonds

225g (8 oz) butter, diced

250g (9 oz) caster sugar

75g (3 oz) chopped almonds

1 large egg, beaten

a few drops of almond essence

350–450g (12–16 oz) raspberries (see above)

To serve:

cream or ice cream

1 Preheat the oven to 180°C/350°F/gas 4. Lightly grease a baking tray 23 cm x 33 cm (9 inches x 13 inches).

2 Put the flour and ground almonds into a food processor, add the butter and the sugar and buzz for a few seconds, until the mixture resembles breadcrumbs. Alternatively, this can be done by hand in a bowl by rubbing the chopped pieces of butter through the flour with your fingertips.

3 Remove 175 g (6 oz) of this mixture and put it into a separate bowl. Add the chopped almonds and set aside.

4 Add the egg and almond essence to the remaining mixture and buzz quickly again (or mix in by hand). The resulting mixture will be rather crumbly. Scatter it over the base of the tin, spreading it out evenly, then pat it down to make a solid base layer with no holes.

5 Spread the raspberries all over the base, but leaving a narrow margin empty all around the edge. Using the mixture you had set aside, scatter it in an even layer over the whole lot.

6 Bake for 45–55 minutes, reducing the temperature if necessary halfway through (to 170°C/325°F/gas 3). Remove from the oven and allow to cool in the tin standing on a wire tray, then cut into approximately 12 pieces. If liked, accompany with cream or ice cream.

Baking Bread

The choice of ready-made breads has multiplied so much over recent years that one need never bake at home. Think carefully before embarking on a home-made bread experience, because once beguiled by the delicious aromas wafting through the house and the absolute freshness and lovely flavour of your own breads and scones, it's easy to get hooked.

Baking bread requires a raising agent (which produces a kind of gas inside the dough) to help it rise in the oven.

Bread Soda

The most popular raising agent in Ireland is bread soda (bicarbonate of soda), an alkali that, when combined with buttermilk (an acid), creates gentle bubbles of gas in the dough and so makes it rise. This happens quickly, so the oven must be heated before starting to mix the dough. Also, because the bubbles are gentle, the dough doesn't need to be tough and so should be handled relatively gently.

Baking Powder

This is a combination of alkali and acid and is used mainly to raise cakes and scones. No buttermilk is required. Once again, the bubbles are gentle and the dough should be handled relatively gently and put into the oven as soon as it's prepared.

Yeast

The rules for using yeast as a raising agent in breads are directly opposite to the rules for using bread soda or baking powder. Strong flour must be used, not self-raising – check the name on the packet. In order to ensure the yeast is well mixed and to toughen the dough so that it will entrap the strong expanding gases made by the yeast, the dough has to be well kneaded for approximately 10 minutes. This could be the perfect antidote to a tough day, but not for me – too lazy by half, I use my strong electric beater with a dough hook while I busy myself with something else in the kitchen.

The high heat of the oven kills the yeast, so most of the rising of the dough (proving) is done in a warm place before going into the oven. However, if left for too long, the dough will collapse. A yeast dough can be frozen until required, then thaw it, shape it, allow to rise and then bake.

Cheese Scones

See photograph, page 235

Makes about 14

Scones are a perfect introduction to home baking, as they cook quickly and are fun to make. Normally I don't bother with a scone cutter, but simply shape the flattened dough into a rectangle and then cut it into squares with a knife. The handling and kneading of scone dough should be light and quick in order not to toughen the flour. The more you make them, the better you'll get at it.

Once cut, avoid handling the cut edges of the scones so they rise evenly. Experiment with various flavourings instead of cheese.

You will need:

450g (1 lb) self-raising flour

110 g (4 oz) butter

salt and freshly ground black pepper

75 g (3 oz) mature cheddar cheese, grated

1 egg and enough milk to make up 225 g (8 fl oz)

1 teaspoon mustard

1   Preheat the oven to 200°C/400°F/gas 6 and lightly grease a baking tray.
2   Put the flour into a bowl and rub in the butter until the mixture resembles fine bread-crumbs (a food processor will do this in seconds), then transfer the mixture to a bowl. Season well with salt and pepper and mix the grated cheese into the flour mixture.
3   In a separate bowl, whisk the egg, milk and mustard together. Add three-quarters of the egg/milk mixture to the dry ingredients and mix through to make a dough that is neither too firm nor too soft, adding more of the liquid only if it's required.
4   Turn the dough out onto a floured board and knead lightly a few times. Turn up the smooth underside and shape into a rectangle about 2.5–3.5 cm (1–1½ inches) thick. Cut into squares with a sharp knife dipped in flour or use a round scone cutter 5 cm (2 inches) in diameter, being sure to cut the scones as close to each other as possible to minimise spare bits of dough. Gather up the leftover bits of dough and reknead them, pressing out once again and cutting. (The scones from this second kneading tend not to be as light as the first lot.)
5   Place the scones on the baking tray and bake for about 15–25 minutes, until risen, golden brown and cooked through. Cool on a wire tray. Serve warm or cold with butter.

Variations:

Scones with herbs and olives

The grated cheese from the recipe above can be included or omitted as required, then also add:

2 tablespoons of chopped fresh herbs (parsley, chives, oregano)
10–12 pitted olives, chopped
1–2 teaspoons green pesto (added to the egg mix)

Scones with blue cheese and toasted walnuts

Omit the grated cheese and instead use 110 g (4 oz) each of blue cheese and toasted chopped walnuts.

Cheese, Garlic and Herb Bread

See photograph, page 45

Serves 4

This is really tasty and satisfying with the chunky chicken soup on p. 49. Bake just prior to serving so that the bread is still crispy. I always cut the slices right through, making it much easier to serve.

You will need:

1 long French baton or 1 fat Vienna bread-style loaf

110 g (4 oz) butter, soft

3 cloves of garlic, crushed

1–2 level tablespoons finely chopped fresh parsley

**1–2 teaspoons chopped fresh herbs (thyme, oregano, etc.) or ½
 teaspoon herbes de Provence or dried oregano**

salt and freshly ground black pepper

75–110 g (3–4 oz) mature cheddar cheese, grated

1 Preheat the oven to 200°C/400°F/gas 6.
2 Cut the bread into slices, cutting right through, but keep the slices in their proper sequence.
3 To make the savoury butter, beat the butter in a bowl, then mix in the crushed garlic, herbs, salt and pepper until they are evenly distributed. Spread the butter generously on one side of each bread slice, then scatter a little cheese on top.
4 Arrange the bread back together again on a large piece of foil (shiny side towards the bread). Spread a final bit of butter over the top of the bread and scatter with the remaining cheese.
5 Brush a separate narrow piece of foil (the same length of the bread) with oil. Place, oiled side down, over the top of the loaf (so that the melted cheese won't stick too much). Close the bottom piece of large foil over the narrow strip to make a parcel.
6 When ready to cook, bake for about 20 minutes. Open the foil and fold back when ready to serve.

Brown Bread in a Casserole

Makes 1 loaf

This idea was inspired by the cast iron pot ovens of old, which were put into a hot turf fire in the open hearth, with more hot turf put on the lid. The lid keeps the steam inside, which results in well-risen bread with a thin, crisp crust that has no cracks around the sides.

The problem with baking the bread on flat tins in a hot oven is that the top crust sets hard before the bread has time to rise properly and so it cracks around the sides. Ideally use a cast iron or Pyrex casserole, though I have successfully used a deep cake tin (23 cm/9 inches) with a sandwich tin inverted on top as a lid. Whatever container you use, it must be preheated in the oven.

The bread soda in the mix gives a nice golden colour to the bread, though too much will result in bread that is too dark and with an unpleasant taste, while too little will yield a pale, insipid one. To give a nice texture and an extra lift to the brown bread, I also include some baking powder. However, you might find that a little trial and error may be necessary to achieve the effect that you want.

You will need:
450 g (1 lb) wholemeal flour
225 g (8 oz) white flour
2 teaspoons bread soda
2 teaspoons baking powder
1 egg, lightly beaten (optional)
425–570 ml (³/₄–1 pint) buttermilk
50g (2 oz) butter, melted (optional)

Optional extras:
75g (3 oz) raisins
50g (2 oz) chopped walnuts

You will also need a casserole with a lid with a 2.8 litre (5 pints) capacity

NOTE: YOU CAN SUBSTITUTE 75G (3 OZ) OAT FLAKES FOR 110 G (4 OZ) OF THE WHOLEMEAL FLOUR.

1 Preheat the oven and the casserole to 200°C/400°F/gas 6.
2 Put all the dry ingredients (including the raisins and nuts if you are using them) into a bowl and mix thoroughly, then make a hole in the centre.
3 In a separate bowl, mix the egg, buttermilk and the melted butter together. Pour most of

the liquid into the dry ingredients. Mix well with a wooden spoon, adding more liquid if necessary to make a medium-soft dough. Shape roughly into a ball in the bowl (see note).

4   Sprinkle some wholemeal flour in the base of the hot casserole and lightly butter the sides. Put in the dough and pat it down to smooth the top and fit the container. Sprinkle a little wholemeal flour over the top. Using a sharp knife, cut a cross 1 cm (^{1}/$_2$ inch) deep from side to side into the top of the bread (this ensures that the bread rises evenly).

5   Cover with the lid and bake for about 50–60 minutes. Avoid opening the lid for as long as you can so that the steam is kept inside. The lid can be lifted quickly to check after about 35 minutes. The bread will brown inside the closed lid, but if liked, remove the lid for the last 5–10 minutes of baking.

6   When properly cooked, the bread will have a hollow sound when rapped on the base with your knuckles. Turn out of the casserole and cool the bread on a wire tray. Eat within a day or two or freeze in sections. This is good toasted.

NOTE: IF YOU PREFER, THE DOUGH CAN BE KNEADED A LITTLE ON A FLOURED BOARD, THEN TURN UP THE SMOOTH UNDERSIDE AND PLACE IN THE HOT CASSEROLE.

Focaccia

Makes 1 wide bread

Focaccia is a flat, savoury Italian bread that can be baked on a flat tin in a round or rectangular shape. It looks attractive with various ingredients baked on the top. Choose those that will give good flavour.

Focaccia is made with a yeast bread dough that is also suitable for making pizza bases. The raw dough can be successfully frozen, so why not make double the amount?

You will need:
700 g (1½ lb) strong white flour
40 g (1½ oz) butter, softened
1 teaspoon salt
1 x 7 g sachet fast-action bread yeast (e.g. McDougalls)
1 egg, beaten
200 ml (7 fl oz) milk
110 ml (4 fl oz) boiling water
110 ml (4 fl oz) cold water

For the toppings:
4 tablespoons olive oil
½ tablespoon lemon juice or balsamic vinegar
½ teaspoon dried oregano
generous pinch of ground coriander
salt and freshly ground black pepper
175 g (6 oz) cherry tomatoes
10–12 black or green pitted olives, halved
a little Maldon sea salt, to sprinkle on top

1 Put the flour, butter, salt and yeast into a bowl.
2 In a separate bowl, mix the egg with the milk. Add the boiling water and then the cold water to make a tepid/warm mixture. Pour the liquid into the dry ingredients and mix well.
3 Knead for a good 5 minutes in an electric mixer with a dough hook or by hand for about 10 minutes. Occasionally cut down the dough off the hook to ensure an even mix. Turn off the mixer, cover the bowl with a damp cloth and leave for about 30 minutes or more, until nearly doubled in size. Remove the cloth and mix or knead again, reducing the dough back to its original size.
4 Roll out the dough and place on a rectangular or round tin. Cover with a lightly oiled plastic bag (ideally, it shouldn't touch the surface of the dough) and leave again in a warm place to double in size.

5 Meanwhile, preheat the oven to 210°C/425°F/gas 7.
6 Prepare the topping ingredients and mix everything (except the Maldon salt) together in a bowl.
7 When the dough is well risen, press little dimples down into the dough with your fingers. Spoon the topping mixture evenly over the top and sprinkle sparingly with the sea salt.
8 Bake for about 30 minutes, until nicely golden. Cool on a wire tray.

Index